Preschooler
Play & Learn

Penny Warner

 Meadowbrook Press

Distributed by Simon & Schuster
New York

Library of Congress Cataloging-in-Publication Data
Warner, Penny.
    Preschooler play & learn / Penny Warner; [illustrations, Jack Lindstrom].
       p. cm.
    Includes index.
    ISBN 0-88166-370-0 (Meadowbrook)—ISBN 0-671-31821-7 (Simon & Schuster)
    1. Play. 2. Education, Preschool—Activity programs. I. Title: Preschooler play
and learn. II. Title.
LB1140.35.P55 W39 1999
372.5—dc21

                                                    00-024630

Managing Editor: Christine Zuchora-Walske
Copyeditor: Joseph Gredler
Proofreader: Liya Lev Oertel
Production Manager: Paul Woods
Desktop Publishing: Danielle White
Illustrations: Jack Lindstrom

Published by Meadowbrook Press, 5451 Smetana Drive, Minnetonka, MN 55343
www.meadowbrookpress.com

BOOK TRADE DISTRIBUTION by Simon & Schuster, a division of Simon and
Schuster, Inc., 1230 Avenue of the Americas, New York, NY 10020

04 03 02 01 00   10 9 8 7 6 5 4 3 2 1

Printed in the United States of America

TABLE OF CONTENTS

INTRODUCTION

Welcome to *Preschooler Play & Learn*. Now that your child is beyond the baby stage, she's ready for even more fun and games during what experts call the "Play Years!" And you, the parent or caregiver, are the very best plaything for your growing child. She learns more from you than any toy. By playing and interacting with you, your child will grow rapidly in all areas of development.

Between the ages of three and six, your child undergoes remarkable changes in:

- **Physical Growth**
  - *Gross Motor Skills:* Your child's body is becoming more flexible. Her arms and legs are lengthening and getting stronger, so she's able to do more gross motor activities such as running, jumping, climbing, rolling, swinging, riding a tricycle—even skating and skiing!
  - *Fine Motor Skills:* As your child's fingers slim down and lengthen, she's better at tasks requiring manual dexterity such as drawing, coloring, feeding herself, dressing herself, tying her shoes, and brushing her teeth.
  - *Coordination and Balance:* Increased coordination of body movements and the ability to retain her balance will open new doors for your child in the areas of simple sports, activities, and advanced play.

PARENTS: We've provided lots of ideas for helping your child develop her physical skills. We've included vigorous games for gross motor development, creative activities for fine motor development, and simple tasks to develop coordination and balance.

- **Cognitive Growth**
  - *Thinking Skills:* As your child's brain develops in size, capacity, and specialty function, her thinking and problem-solving abilities improve dramatically. She's able to reason more concretely, seek solutions to tasks, and remember things in greater detail for longer periods of time.

PARENTS: We'll help you challenge your child with interesting tasks that stimulate brain development and enable your child to practice thinking skills during fun games and activities.

- **Language Skills**
  - *Symbolic Thinking:* Your child's language skills are exploding during this period. As her cognitive ability grows, she begins to think symbolically through the use of language. She substitutes words for pictures and gestures, and she

understands the meanings of hundreds of concepts. She uses words to express needs, share feelings, and interact socially.

- *Vocabulary:* At age six your child will probably have a vocabulary of over ten thousand words, will understand the basic rules of grammar, and will increase her vocabulary by six to ten new words each day!

PARENTS: We've suggested numerous techniques for enhancing your child's language development through word games, exciting conversation topics, simple rhymes, and repetition activities. We've also provided prereading and prewriting tasks that will eventually lead to your child's success in school.

- **Psychological Growth**
  - *Self-Awareness:* As your child grows physically and cognitively, she also becomes aware of her identity. She recognizes her body parts, shows off her toys, draws simple pictures of herself and her family, and enjoys saying her name and age.
  - *Self-Confidence and Self-Esteem:* Along with self-awareness comes self-confidence, which leads to self-esteem. As your child begins to know herself better, she gains confidence in her ability to try new things, take chances, and complete tasks. Each success promotes her self-esteem, which leads to further challenges and successes.

PARENTS: We've offered fun ways to help your child learn more about herself through physical activities, art, and social interaction. And we've included tips to help her gain self-confidence and self-esteem through interactive games and activities that focus on success.

- **Emotional Expression**
  - *Sharing Feelings:* Psychologically, your child is well past the reflex crying stage and can more appropriately express her feelings, desires, wants, and needs. As her emotions become more fine-tuned and controlled, she's better able to manage her feelings through verbalizing, art expression, and dramatic play.

PARENTS: We've provided plenty of tips on how to help your child express her emotions in positive ways. Since your child loves playing make-believe, we've provided activities to help her express, channel, and act out her feelings through imaginary and dramatic fun.

- **Social Skills**
  - *Social Interaction:* Your child's social skills increase as she comes in contact with more people at home and in the neighborhood and community. Getting along with others is crucial to success in all areas of life, so your child should spend lots of time with friends and peers.

PARENTS: You'll find plenty of age-appropriate activities to help your child learn social skills through dramatic play, taking turns, and playing games involving sharing and cooperation.

By providing a stimulating educational environment, you as a parent or caregiver can help your child reach her developmental potential. Just remember:

1. Your child learns through play, especially when you are actively involved.
2. You're the best teacher for your child, and you can make learning fun.
3. Enjoy spending time with your child. The investment will pay off in more ways than you can imagine.

All you need are a few stimulating ideas, some creative materials, and time to enjoy the fun. And we're here to help! In *Preschooler Play & Learn* you'll find:

- 150 games and activities for hours of challenges and rewards.
- Recommended ages for each game and activity.
- A list of easy-to-find materials needed for each game and activity.
- Step-by-step instructions for each game and activity.
- Variations for added fun and enhanced learning.
- Safety tips to make sure your child doesn't get hurt while playing.
- A list of skills your child is learning through each activity.

So have fun with your preschooler during the Play Years, and enjoy the change from clumsy to graceful, from few words to a rich vocabulary, and from an egocentric toddler to a socially adept human being. The bond you build with your child during these years will last forever.

3 TO 3½ YEARS

Welcome to the Thoughtful Threes! Your child is becoming taller and leaner as he emerges from the toddler years. Along with the changes in his body come dramatic changes in his physical skills:

- Your child's motor coordination is fine-tuning itself as he moves his arms, legs, hands, and fingers while performing specific tasks. Provide him with lots of opportunities to practice his gross and fine motor skills indoors and out.

- Your child is becoming more adept at physical tasks and gaining the confidence to try new things—and he thinks he can do just about anything! Give him plenty of opportunities to succeed and further enhance his self-esteem.

- Your child is experiencing a new freedom of locomotion. He's learning to move his body through space in creative ways, not only by walking, but by running, hopping, jumping, rolling, dancing, climbing, and leaping. Make sure he has lots of open space in which to practice these skills.

- Your child's developing fine motor skills are allowing him to do more challenging tasks such as drawing, coloring, painting, cutting, and pasting. Give him materials to use so he can fine-tune his manual dexterity.

ANIMAL PARTS

Have your child match the heads and tails of various animals. Or, let her have fun making crazy new animals!

Materials:
- Pictures of animals from magazines or inexpensive picture books
- Scissors
- Glue or paste
- Sheets of construction paper
- Floor or table

Learning Skills:	• Body image • Classification skills • Cognitive/thinking skills • Fine motor development

What to Do:

1. Cut out pictures of various animals.

2. Cut the pictures in half, separating the head area from the tail area.

3. Place the head halves on the floor or table in front of your child.

4. Pull out one of the tail halves and let her match it to the appropriate head.

5. Have her glue each completed animal onto a sheet of construction paper.

6. Repeat until all the animals are reconnected.

Variation: Have your child intentionally mismatch the heads and tails to create funny new animals!

Caution: Put away the scissors after you cut up the pictures, and make sure your child doesn't put glue in her mouth.

ANiMAL WALK

Your child will have fun walking just like the animals! Help him use his imagination to move his arms, legs, head, and body.

Materials:
- Large room
- Picture books that include animals with distinct walks such as ducks, crabs, frogs, kangaroos, elephants, inchworms, chickens, rabbits, seals, snakes, caterpillars, and so on

Learning Skills:	• Classification skills • Dramatic play • Emotional expression • Gross motor development • Social skills

What to Do:

1. Leaf through various picture books about animals.

2. As you read, encourage your child to try to walk like the animals in the books.

3. Help him by describing the movements and demonstrating if necessary. For example, show him how the duck waddles, the crab moves sideways, the kangaroo leaps, the elephant lumbers, the inchworm inches, the chicken lunges, the rabbit hops, the seal slides, the snake slithers, and the caterpillar...does a caterpillar walk!

Variation: Take turns imitating an animal walk and have the other person guess what animal you are!

Caution: Make sure the area is clear of obstacles.

3

BACK WORDS

Your child's language skills are exploding, so encourage her to have fun with words by giving them a new twist. Say sentences and phrases backwards!

Materials:
• Mealtime setting

What to Do:

Learning Skills:	• Cognitive/thinking skills • Emotional expression • Language and vocabulary development • Sequencing • Social interaction

1. Play during mealtime, so your child can learn the game while using familiar sentences.

2. Start with simple sentences like "More milk please" and "Thank you." Say them backwards: "Please milk more" and "You thank."

3. Demonstrate a few times so she understands how to play.

4. Progress to longer sentences as your child gets better at playing the game.

Variation: Have a backwards hour when you do and say everything backwards. Or, try acting out a scene from a favorite book together backwards!

Caution: If your child becomes frustrated because she can't understand the game, try using two-word sentences only, or stop and try again a few days later.

BOX CAR

A simple box can turn a child into a creative genius who can learn to do wonderful things with his mind and body!

Materials:
- Large box about half the size of your child
- Scissors or X-acto knife
- Duct tape
- Felt-tip pens, crayons, paint, stickers, decals, fringe, and other decorative materials
- Book about cars and trucks

Learning Skills:	• Body awareness • Creativity and imagination • Fine and gross motor development • Spatial relationships

What to Do:

1. Read a book about cars and trucks together and study the pictures.

2. Cut the top and bottom off a large box, leaving the sides intact.

3. Use duct tape to cover any rough edges and to reinforce corners, if needed.

4. Help your child decorate the outside of the box to look like a car or truck using felt-tip pens, paint, stickers, and so on.

5. When the car is finished, let your child take a drive around the house or yard.

6. For added fun, set up roads by laying down rope as a guide, and set up stop signs along the route.

Variation: Make an airplane or boat instead of a car, and let your child fly away or set sail!

Caution: Use caution with the scissors or X-acto knife with your child close by.

5

CAN YOU GUESS?

If you provide enough clues, your child will guess what you're thinking about in no time at all! Give her a chance to quiz you, too!

Materials:
• Room with interesting items

What to Do:
1. Select an interesting and easily visible item, such as a figurine, located in the room.

Learning Skills:	• Classification skills • Cognitive/thinking skills • Language and vocabulary development • Mental imaging • Problem solving

2. Tell your child you're thinking about something in the room and give her a clue such as the color, size, or shape.

3. Have her try to guess the item.

4. If your child guesses incorrectly, give her another clue and let her guess again.

5. Continue until she guesses the item.

6. Let your child take a turn choosing something and providing clues for you!

Variation: This is a great game to play while driving or waiting in line.

Caution: Be sure the item remains visible at all times. Also, don't choose any items that are potentially dangerous to your child.

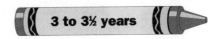

CAR-WASH BATH

Even kids who hate baths love the Car-Wash Bath—and they learn something while getting clean!

Materials:
- Bathtub
- Bubble bath
- Eye goggles
- Sponges and washcloths
- Shampoo and soap
- Sprayers and squirters
- Towels
- Lotion

Learning Skills:	• Body awareness • Cognitive/thinking skills • Creativity and imagination • Gross motor development

What to Do:

1. Fill the tub with warm water.

2. Add bubble bath as the tub fills.

3. Place your child in the tub and fit goggles over his eyes.

4. Sponge him all over with sponges and washcloths.

5. Shampoo his hair and lather him up with soap.

6. Spray him clean with squirters, just like in the car wash!

7. Towel him off.

8. Wax him with lotion. All clean!

Variation: Follow the same procedure in the shower. Your child can go through the car wash there, too!

Caution: Make sure to keep soap out of your child's eyes. Also, make sure the water isn't too hot and watch that he doesn't slip in the tub. *Never leave your child unattended in the bathtub.*

7

COLOR MY HAND

Help your child learn the parts of the body by creating a coloring book of her own body parts! Begin with her hand, then work up her arm to her elbows and face, then down to the stomach, legs, knees, and feet.

Materials:
- Photocopy machine
- Felt-tip pens or crayons

Learning Skills:	• Body awareness • Classification skills • Eye-hand coordination • Fine motor development • Self-esteem

What to Do:

1. Place your child's hand on the glass surface of a photocopy machine.

2. Cover her hand with the copier flap.

3. Tell her to close her eyes while the machine makes a copy so the bright light doesn't hurt her eyes.

4. Press the button to make a copy.

5. Take the copy home. If the copy quality is poor, outline the hand with a black felt-tip pen before having her color it with felt-tip pens or crayons.

6. Let her add whatever details she wants such as rings, fingernails, nail polish, bracelets, and so on.

Variation: Photocopy lots of body parts and have your child put them together when you get home. She can color the pictures and see what kind of funny person she turns out to be!

Caution: Make sure your child closes her eyes while the machine is copying. Protect yourself the same way.

FOLLOW THE STICKERS

Here's a version of a treasure hunt that keeps your child searching for the trail. Where it leads is up to you!

Materials:
- Dozen or more colorful stickers
- Treat such as a cracker or small toy
- Large play area

Learning Skills:	• Cognitive/thinking skills • Gross motor development • Imagination • Problem solving • Visual discrimination/ visual tracking

What to Do:

1. Buy a pack of colorful stickers.

2. Design a trail for your child to follow through the house or backyard.

3. Position stickers in plain sight every few feet along the trail.

4. Place a treat or toy at the end.

5. Have your child enter the search area and explain that he has to look for a trail of stickers that will lead to a treat.

6. Congratulate him when he finally discovers his prize!

Variation: To make the hunt more challenging, position the stickers farther apart each time you play. Also, have your child design a sticker trail for you! He can plan the entire route and choose the treat.

Caution: Avoid having your child climb up high or go near dangerous objects.

GO TOGETHER?

Teach your child to match items that go together, then see if she can make up a matching game for you!

Materials:
- Items that go together such as a shoe and sock, pencil and paper, fork and plate, soap and washcloth, toothpaste and toothbrush, comb and ribbon, ketchup and mustard, and so on
- Floor or table

Learning Skills:
- Classification skills
- Cognitive/thinking skills
- Language and vocabulary development
- Matching skills

What to Do:

1. Gather several pairs of items that go together but that are not identical.

2. Separate the pairs of items into two piles.

3. Place the first pile on the floor or table in front of your child.

4. Bring out one of the matching items from the other pile and show it to your child.

5. Have her select the matching item.

6. Set the matched pair off to the side and select another item.

7. Continue until all the items are paired.

8. Discuss how the items go together and how they are different.

9. Give your child a turn collecting matching items for you to pair!

Variation: Place all the items on the floor or table and let your child choose which ones go together.

Caution: Be sure the items are safe to handle.

GUESS THE END

Teach your child how to anticipate the ending of a story. He'll be able to apply this skill to all kinds of cognitive tasks, especially problem solving.

Materials:
• Picture book with an exciting ending

What to Do:
1. Find a cozy place to read the book.

2. Read part of the story to your child, stopping before you get to the end.

Learning Skills:	• Cognitive/thinking skills • Creativity and imagination • Language and vocabulary development • Problem solving • Sequencing

3. Ask him what he thinks will happen.

4. Encourage him to think of several possible endings.

5. Read the rest of the book to find out how the story ends.

6. Discuss with him how the actual ending compares to the ones he imagined.

7. Repeat with other books.

Variation: Watch the first part of a movie. Repeat the procedure above, stopping in the middle to discuss possible endings.

Caution: It's a good idea to select books that have happy endings, where problems are solved and the solutions are satisfying. Your child might become frustrated otherwise.

HANDY DANDY

Have your child use her imagination to see what she can create out of a tracing of her own hand!

Materials:
- Sheets of paper
- Felt-tip pens

Learning Skills:	• Body image • Creativity and imagination • Fine motor development • Self-esteem/self-awareness

What to Do:

1. Trace outlines of your child's hand on several sheets of paper.

2. Have her color the hands, turning them into anything she likes such as a turkey, rooster, flower garden, face with big hair, sunrise, funny monster, porcupine, and so on.

3. See how many different things she can make from her hand outline!

Variation: Make foot drawings, too, and see what your child can make from them.

Caution: Use nontoxic, child-safe pens.

DiFFERENT SOUNDS

Teach your child how to discriminate between different sounds, especially ones that sound alike. He'll end up being a good listener if he plays this game!

Materials:
- Several pairs of different-sounding items from various categories:
  - –2 appliances: can opener and blender
  - –2 bells: doorbell and telephone
  - –2 musical instruments: piano and guitar
  - –2 animals: dog and cat
  - –2 toys: bouncing ball and stacking block
- Cassette recorder and tape
- Table

Learning Skills:	• Attention span • Classification skills • Cognitive/thinking skills • Listening skills/auditory discrimination • Mental imaging

What to Do:

1. Find several pairs of related items and tape-record their sounds.

2. Place the smaller items on a table.

3. Have your child listen to the tape and point to the item that is making the sound. He may have to move around the house to find larger items such as the piano or the animals. Stop the tape if he needs more time and repeat sounds if necessary.

4. After your child identifies all the sounds, separate the items into pairs and talk about how they sound similar and how they sound different.

Variation: Don't display any of the items on a table, and have your child guess each one as it plays on the tape. Or, play only one of the sounds, let him point to the item, then have him choose another item that makes a similar sound.

Caution: Make sure the tape recorder volume isn't too loud and avoid scary sounds.

MAKE A BOOK

Encourage your child to tell a story and make her own book, just like the real books at the library!

Materials:
- Children's magazines or inexpensive picture books
- Paper, glue, tape, scissors, and stapler
- Felt-tip pens

Learning Skills:
- Cognitive/thinking skills
- Creativity and imagination
- Language and vocabulary development
- Sequencing

What to Do:

1. Cut out eight to ten pictures from children's magazines or picture books.

2. Lay out all the pictures on the floor so you can see them.

3. Glue the pictures (one per page) to plain sheets of paper, leaving enough room at the bottom to write a few lines of a story.

4. Have your child choose one picture, then another, and so on until all the pictures have been collected into a stack.

5. Place a plain sheet of paper on top of the stack and staple the pages together.

6. Have your child look at the first picture and begin telling a story that somehow relates to the picture's contents.

7. Write down what she says under the picture.

8. Turn the page and have her look at the second picture and continue telling the story while you write down what she says under the picture.

9. Continue until you reach the end of the book.

10. Have her create a title and write it on the top sheet.

11. Read the story together!

Variation: Have your child tell a story while you write it down. Then have her draw pictures to fit the story. Retell the story when the book is finished.

Caution: Be careful with the stapler and scissors as you work. Also, you might want to tape-record her story and write it down later.

ME DOLL

What child wouldn't like a paper doll that looks just like him? He'll probably want to play with dolls of other family members, too!

Materials:
- Package of paper dolls
- Photo of your child
- Pictures of family members (optional)
- Glue
- Scissors

Learning Skills:
- Body awareness
- Creativity and imagination
- Language and vocabulary development
- Self-image/self-esteem
- Social skills

What to Do:

1. Buy a package of paper dolls appropriate for your child's age.

2. Cut out the head portion of your child's photo.

3. Glue this portion over the doll's head.

4. Make paper dolls of other family members, too, if your child likes.

5. Let your child enjoy playing with the paper dolls!

Variation: Have your child perform a puppet show with the paper dolls, telling a story about home life!

Caution: Handle the scissors and glue carefully around your child.

PEEK A BiT

Can your child guess the secret item while only peeking a little bit? The more she sees, the easier it is to figure out!

Materials:
- Several large items that are interesting to look at such as a stuffed animal, article of clothing, picture book, toy car, baby doll, puzzle, and so on
- Large paper bag to hold the items
- Cloth, towel, or small blanket

Learning Skills:	• Classification skills • Cognitive/thinking skills • Mental imaging • Problem solving

What to Do:

1. Collect several items and place them in a paper bag.

2. Reach into the bag with a cloth and remove one item, keeping it covered all the time.

3. Set the cloth-covered item between you and your child.

4. Carefully reveal a small portion of the item.

5. Have your child try to guess the item.

6. Continue showing more and more until she guesses correctly.

7. Repeat with the other items in the bag.

Variation: To make it easier, show your child the items before putting them in the bag. To make it more challenging, use only pictures of the items.

Caution: Choose items that are safe for your child to handle.

RHYMING RHYTHM

Help your child keep the beat and learn more language at the same time! This game takes some coordination, but it makes talking lots of fun!

Materials:
• Music (optional)

What to Do:

1. Think of a word that is easy to rhyme with such as "goat."

Learning Skills:	• Coordination and rhythm
	• Emotional expression
	• Language and vocabulary development
	• Listening skills
	• Social interaction

2. Begin clapping your hands slowly, encouraging your child to maintain your rhythm.

3. Say the word while you clap your hands.

4. Have your child say a rhyming word while you continue to clap.

5. Maintain the clapping rhythm while he thinks of more rhyming words. You could also take turns coming up with rhyming words until you run out.

6. Choose a new word and play again.

Variation: Play music and say the rhyming words to the beat of the music.

Caution: Watch out for bad words!

SCARF DANCING

It's amazing what a few scarves can do to release a child's creativity and improve her gross motor skills. Turn on music and watch the scarves fly!

Materials:
- 2 long scarves, at least as long as your child's height
- 2 chopsticks or similar sticks
- Large area
- Cassette player with music

Learning Skills:	• Coordination • Creativity and imagination • Emotional expression • Gross motor development • Spatial relationships

What to Do:

1. Tie one end of each scarf to the end of a chopstick.

2. Turn on some music.

3. Have your child hold one stick in each hand and begin waving the scarves around.

4. As she waves them to the music, encourage her to move her body to make the scarves move even more.

5. Have her choreograph a simple scarf dance to go with the music.

Variation: Hold one scarf stick while she holds the other and dance together. Intertwine the scarves from time to time and see what happens!

Caution: Make sure obstacles are moved out of the way. Don't tie the scarf to your child—she might get tangled up and fall.

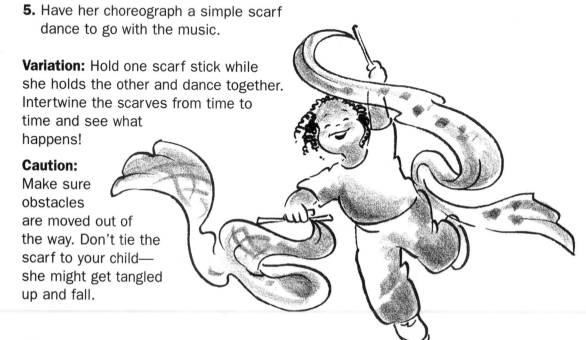

SKIP, HOP, AND JUMP

Your child must listen carefully to a few simple instructions, or he'll end up skipping when he should have hopped or jumped!

Materials:
• Large area

What to Do:

1. Stand in a large, obstacle-free area where your child has plenty of room to perform the tasks.

Learning Skills:	• Body awareness • Coordination and reflexes • Gross motor development • Language and vocabulary development • Listening/auditory discrimination

2. Call out one of the commands—skip, hop, or jump—and have him respond accordingly.

3. Call out another command and have him switch to that task.

4. Continue calling out commands, but begin going faster and faster until he breaks into giggles and collapses!

5. Play again, and add more commands such as dance, twirl, leap, and so on.

Variation: Take a stroll through your neighborhood and call out different types of walking as you go such as slow, fast, backwards, sideways, baby steps, giant steps, skip, hop, jump, and so on. Or, change your walking style as you go and have your child copy you!

Caution: If your child gets confused or frustrated, slow down the commands or stop the game.

TALK AND TAPE

Kids love to hear the sounds of their own voices, so tape-record your child's speech and play it back. See how many different ways she can make herself sound!

Materials:
- Cassette recorder
- Microphone
- Blank tape

Learning Skills:	• Cognitive/thinking skills • Creativity and imagination • Language and vocabulary development • Listening skills

What to Do:

1. Place a blank tape in the cassette recorder.

2. Choose an interesting topic for your child to talk about such as "What did you do at preschool?" "What do you want for your birthday?" or "What happened on your favorite TV show?"

3. Turn on the tape, hold the microphone close to her mouth, and let her talk about the subject.

4. Play the tape back and listen to her voice together!

5. Pick another topic and have her speak again, but this time have her use a different voice such as very low, very high, a cartoon character, and so on.

6. Have your child change voices for each topic, then listen to the entire tape from the beginning.

Variation: Tape-record family members and friends and see if your child can guess who's talking!

Caution: If the cassette player plugs into an outlet, tell your child not to touch the cord. Also, make sure she's careful with the recorder buttons.

TiPPY TAP

Have some finger fun with a game of Tippy Tap. Have your child make his fingers do the talking, walking, and tapping!

Materials:
- 10 small thimbles or pen caps
- Hard surface

Learning Skills:	• Body awareness • Coordination • Fine motor development • Listening/auditory discrimination • Math/counting skills

What to Do:
1. Cover your child's fingertips with thimbles or pen caps. You might need to cover his fingertips with small Band-Aids first, so the thimbles or pen caps fit snugly.

2. Have your child tap a rhythm on a hard surface such as a table.

3. Play some music and have him keep time to the tune with his tapping.

4. Have him tap his fingers on various objects around the room and listen to the different sounds he can make.

Variation: Take a turn wearing the thimbles and tap a tune on different areas of your body. Have him close his eyes and guess what body part you're tapping by sound alone!

Caution: Don't use sharp-pointed pen tops, and make sure your child doesn't put the tappers in his mouth. Also, don't let your child tap on glass or other easily breakable objects.

TOE TAPPERS

Kids love to hear themselves talk, and, with this game, they will also love to hear themselves walk! Make it easy for your child to hear her sounds with twinkling Toe Tappers!

Materials:
- Old, worn pair of shoes, preferably your child's size
- 8 flat metal washers
- Superglue
- Hard surface

Learning Skills:	• Body awareness • Coordination • Emotional expression • Gross motor development • Spatial relationships

What to Do:

1. Find a worn pair of your child's shoes that are about to be thrown out, or buy a pair at a thrift shop.

2. Superglue four flat metal washers to the bottom of each shoe, two at the toe and two at the heel. Allow to dry.

3. Slip the shoes onto your child's feet and let her walk around on a hard surface.

4. Put on some music and have her tap a rhythm to fit the tune!

Variation: Buy some used tap shoes and let her experience the real thing.

Caution: Make sure your child doesn't walk on slippery surfaces, and have her be extra careful if the shoes don't fit perfectly. Be careful with the superglue.

TIPPITY...
TAP...
TAP!

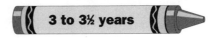

TOUCH AND TELL

Help your child learn to use his sense of touch to explore his environment. Encourage him to make mental pictures of the things he feels.

Materials:
- Several palm-sized items that will feel different to your child such as a stuffed animal, washcloth, cup, cracker, ball, and so on
- Paper bag
- Blindfold (optional)

Learning Skills:	• Classification skills • Fine motor development • Manual dexterity • Mental imaging • Problem solving

What to Do:
1. Collect several differently textured or shaped items and place them in a paper bag.

2. Sit opposite your child on the floor.

3. Blindfold him or ask him to close his eyes.

4. Remove an item from the bag and place it in your child's hands.

5. Ask him to feel the item carefully and guess what it is.

6. Provide hints if he has trouble guessing correctly.

Variation: To make the game easier, show your child the items before you blindfold him, then follow the instructions above.

Caution: If your child doesn't like blindfolds, have him close his eyes and encourage him not to peek. Make sure the items are safe to touch.

WHAT HAPPENED?

Help your child learn to anticipate and solve problems—before real problems come along! Make it fun for her to figure out solutions.

Materials:
• Picture book with a good story

What to Do:
1. Select a picture book in which events happen that your child can anticipate.

Learning Skills:	• Cognitive/thinking skills • Creativity and imagination • Language and vocabulary development • Problem solving • Sequencing

2. Sit together in a comfortable chair and begin reading the story.

3. As you proceed, ask your child what she thinks is going to happen next and let her guess before you turn the page.

4. Turn the page, read the next part of the story, and see if she was right!

5. Continue until you reach the end of the book.

Variation: Instead of using picture books, find magazine pictures and make up stories to fit the scenes. Begin by asking her, "What happened?"

Caution: Be sure to select books that don't cause your child anxiety about what's going to happen such as a story about death.

WHAT'S MISSING?

It's fun for your child to figure out what's missing, especially when you choose interesting items!

Materials:
- Group of 4 to 6 items such as a toy, snack, book, piece of clothing, and so on
- Floor or table
- Blanket or towel

Learning Skills:
- Classification skills
- Cognitive/thinking skills
- Language and vocabulary development
- Problem solving
- Social interaction

What to Do:

1. Set the items on the floor or table in front of your child.

2. After he examines them, identify them out loud, one at a time.

3. Cover the items with a blanket or towel.

4. Review the names of the items.

5. Take away one item without letting your child see.

6. Remove the blanket and name the items still present.

7. Ask your child, "What's missing?"

8. Repeat steps 4 through 7, removing another item.

9. Gather a new batch of items and play again.

Variation: To make the game more challenging, you can use more items, choose ones more closely related, or skip the review step. To make the game easier, reduce the number of items or review them several times.

Caution: Be sure the items are safe to handle.

WHOSE CLOTHES?

Your child is still learning how to distinguish between boys, girls, men, and women, and this game will help.

Materials:
- Magazines containing pictures of people
- Scissors
- Floor or table

Learning Skills:	• Body image • Classification/thinking skills • Creativity and imagination • Fine motor development • Self-esteem/self-awareness

What to Do:

1. Cut out magazine pictures of men, women, boys, and girls.

2. Then cut out pictures of clothes for the men, women, boys, and girls.

3. Set the pictures of people on the floor or table in front of your child.

4. Set the pictures of clothes nearby.

5. Pick up the first picture of clothing and hand it to your child.

6. Ask her to match it to the man, woman, boy, or girl.

7. Continue until all the clothes have been matched to the people.

Variation: Have your child help you sort the laundry and identify what items belong to each family member!

Caution: Be careful with the scissors around your child.

3½ TO 4 YEARS

Your child's cognitive skills are increasing dramatically. She now thinks more concretely than she did during the "here and now" baby/toddler years. The cognitive theorist Jean Piaget called this stage of intellectual growth "preoperational thought." Here are some examples of your child's cognitive development:

- Your child can now use symbols, particularly language, to express ideas, thoughts, and feelings. That's a huge leap from the primarily gesturing stage of the toddler years. Her rapidly growing vocabulary and language skills enable her to communicate more complex ideas. This helps her better control her world and herself. As parent or caregiver, you should provide her with lots of opportunities to use her language skills and enhance her vocabulary.

- Your child is *egocentric*, but the term does not mean selfish. Piaget used this term to explain that your child is learning to see things from *her* perspective— distinct from her parents'. Your child will sometimes have difficulty seeing things from other people's points of view, so help her try to see other viewpoints as you play together.

- Your child is learning to make her own decisions as she becomes more independent. Her decisions may occasionally conflict with yours, but you should nevertheless encourage your child to think independently by providing her with options and allowing her to make choices.

ALL-ABOUT-ME BOOK

Help your child create a very special book—one starring himself!

Materials:
- Sheets of white paper
- Magazines with pictures
- Photos of your child and other family members
- Samples of your child's artwork
- Scissors
- Glue
- Pen
- Stapler

Learning Skills:	• Cognitive/thinking skills • Emotional expression • Fine motor development • Self-esteem/self-aware-ness

What to Do:

1. Gather visual items that are important to your child, including his artwork, favorite magazine pictures, family photos, and so on.

2. Glue each item onto a sheet of plain paper.

3. Have him describe the significance of each picture, and write that information at the bottom of the page.

4. Staple the pages together and add a title page that reads "All About Me!"

5. Read the book together when it's finished.

Variation: Your child can add pages to the book whenever he likes. He might even want to organize it into chapters.

Caution: Have copies made of precious family photos that you don't want damaged. Be careful with scissors around your child.

ANiMAKER

Have your child create her own species of animals and see what crazy critters she comes up with!

Materials:
- Pictures of animals from magazines or inexpensive picture books
- Scissors
- Paper
- Glue or tape
- Table

Learning Skills:	• Classification skills • Cognitive/thinking skills • Creativity and imagination • Fine motor development

What to Do:
1. Cut out pictures of various animals.

2. Cut the animal pictures into distinct body parts such as the head, torso, legs, tail, and so on.

3. Have your child mix the body parts on a table.

4. Then have her select various body parts to create new animals.

5. Help her glue or tape the body parts in any order she likes onto a sheet of paper.

6. Repeat until all or most of the parts have been used.

7. Help your child name the animals she created.

Variation: Have your child draw her own new animals using only her imagination.

Caution: Be careful with the glue and scissors around your child.

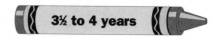

BUBBLE BATH BLOW

Help your child begin to learn the interesting properties of water while he's having fun and getting clean!

Materials:
- Bathtub
- Bubble solution

Learning Skills:	• Cause and effect • Eye-hand coordination • Fine and gross motor development • Scientific properties

What to Do:

1. Fill a tub with warm water and place your child in the tub.

2. Open a bottle of bubble solution and blow some bubbles over the tub. Encourage your child to pop the bubbles before they hit the water.

3. Pour some bubble solution into the water, give your child a straw, and see if he can make bubbles by blowing into the bath water.

Variation: Blow bubbles outside and try to catch them!

Caution: The tub will become slippery with the bubble solution, so be careful getting your child out of the tub. Also, make sure he doesn't inhale the bubble water while blowing.

CATCH THE COLORED CUBES

Your child can learn important new skills anywhere—even in the bathtub while she's getting clean!

Materials:
- Bathtub full of warm water
- Food coloring
- Ice cube tray

Learning Skills:	• Cognitive/thinking skills • Fine motor development • Problem solving • Scientific properties • Sensory exploration

What to Do:

1. Prepare colored ice cubes by adding food coloring to water in an ice cube tray. Freeze the cubes well ahead of bath time.

2. Fill a tub with warm water.

3. Place your child in the tub.

4. Drop the colored ice cubes in the water, a few at a time, and encourage your child to catch them. The slippery cubes will begin to melt in the warm water, so she has to catch them quickly!

5. Continue adding the ice cubes until they're all gone.

6. If necessary, add warm water periodically to keep the tub warm.

Variation: Place a small toy on top of a floating ice cube and see how long it takes the toy to sink! Or, freeze a small toy inside an ice cube for a fun surprise.

Caution: Watch your child at all times in the bath, and make sure the water remains warm.

CHANGE A STORY

Children enjoy anticipating what comes next in a story. Have some fun by changing the story from what your child expects and see if he catches you!

Materials:
- Picture book with an interesting story such as *Where the Wild Things Are, Curious George, Clifford,* or *Arthur*
- Cozy chair

Learning Skills:	• Anticipation/surprise • Cognitive/thinking skills • Creativity and imagination • Mental imaging • Problem solving

What to Do:

1. Find a picture book that tells an exciting story.

2. Sit with your child in a cozy chair and begin the story.

3. As you read, change some of the words so that they no longer fit the illustrations. For example, when Curious George puts on the man's yellow hat, call it a red hat instead.

4. Pause after you make the change and wait for your child's reaction. He should notice that you've read something different from what he expected.

5. If he doesn't speak up, ask him if what you read was correct.

6. Let him think about it and eventually realize the change.

7. Have him make the correction, if possible.

8. Turn the page and change something else about the story.

9. Continue until you finish the story.

Variation: Have your child tell you the story, changing whatever words he likes, and see if you can pick out his changes!

Caution: Choose a book that isn't too scary.

NO!...WRONG!

COLOR WALK

To help your child learn her colors, take a Color Walk and see all the colors that sorround you everywhere you go.

Materials:
• Room, yard, or park full of colors

Learning Skills:
• Classification skills
• Cognitive/thinking skills
• Color concepts
• Gross motor development
• Social skills

What to Do:

1. Invite your child to take a walk with you.

2. As you walk, have her choose a color.

3. Then have her locate as many items as possible that match the color.

4. After she finds ten items, have her select a new color and repeat.

Variation: To make the activity more challenging, each of you can select a different color before starting your walk. The first person to find ten items of her selected color gets to choose the next two colors!

Caution: Watch where you walk to avoid tripping while you're looking for all those colors!

RED!

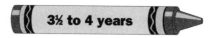

DOES-A-DO?

This game encourages both cognitive and physical development at the same time.

Materials:
- A number of objects that do something such as a rope, ball, blanket, block, spoon, hat, towel, and so on
- Cleared floor area

Learning Skills:	• Body awareness • Cognitive/thinking skills • Gross and fine motor development • Social interaction • Spatial awareness

What to Do:

1. Collect several items that do something.

2. Set them on the floor between you and your child.

3. Select one item (for example, a ball) and ask your child, "What does a ball do?"

4. Have him tell you what the object does, then encourage him to show you what it does!

5. See if he can think of more than one thing the object can do. For example, a ball is bounced, caught, thrown, sat on, rolled, flattened, kicked, carried, and so on.

6. Select the next object and repeat.

Variation: Let your child take a turn choosing a few objects, and then you explain what they do. Don't forget to demonstrate, too!

Caution: Be sure all the objects you use are safe to handle.

34

DOUBLE TALK

Here's a fun way to double your child's language skills: a conversation full of Double Talk.

Materials:
- Topics to discuss such as your child's day at preschool, her favorite book or TV show, her new toy, and so on

Learning Skills:	• Cognitive/thinking skills • Language and vocabulary development • Self-awareness • Social interaction

What to Do:
1. Pick a topic to discuss with your child.

2. Have her begin to tell you a story, one sentence or phrase at a time.

3. Ask her to stop after each sentence or phrase, so you can repeat her words as closely as possible.

4. Continue with the story until she finishes.

5. Reverse roles, with you telling the story and her repeating your words as closely as possible.

Variation: Have her say a couple of sentences and wait for you to repeat them. Reverse the roles. Increase the number of sentences as she gets better and better. Add more words to make the game more challenging.

Caution: If your child doesn't like the copying part, explain again what you're doing and give it another try, or stop the game and try again in a few days.

THE DOGGIE BARKED...

THE DOGGIE BARKED.

FLASHLiGHT TAG

Here's a fun game to play in the dark, and it also teaches spatial awareness.

Materials:
- 2 flashlights
- Dark room

Learning Skills:	• Body awareness
	• Cognitive/thinking skills
	• Gross motor development
	• Social skills
	• Spatial awareness

What to Do:

1. Give your child a flashlight and keep one for yourself.

2. Go into a room and turn off the lights.

3. Have your child turn on his flashlight and try to catch you with the light as you move around the room,

4. After he catches you, you're it! Now it's your turn to catch your child with your flashlight.

Variation: Hide an object in the dark room and see if your child can find it with his flashlight. Give him some clues if necessary!

Caution: Be careful that your child doesn't become afraid of the dark, and clear the area of obstacles.

FOLLOW THE ROPE

Have your child follow a rope that will lead her to mysterious places!

Materials:
- Long length of rope, string, or yarn

Learning Skills:	• Balance/coordination • Body awareness • Cognitive/thinking skills • Gross motor development • Spatial awareness

What to Do:
1. Select a long length of rope, string, or yarn.

2. Lay the rope on the ground or floor from one end of the room or yard to the other.

3. Twist and turn the rope to make it go over, under, and around several obstacles.

4. Ask your child to step on the rope and follow it from the beginning to the end of the path.

5. Tell her not to fall off, or she'll have to start over again!

Variation: After your child completes the path, have her walk the rope backwards.

Caution: Be sure the rope doesn't go over any obstacles that could cause your child to fall and get hurt.

HATS OFF

It's amazing how a simple hat can change a personality! Watch what happens to your child when you put a hat on his head!

Materials:
- Variety of hats from a thrift shop or costume shop such as a baseball cap, feathery hat, scarf, cowboy hat, clown hat, chef's hat, firefighter's helmet, magician's hat, Mickey Mouse hat, and so on
- Mirror

Learning Skills:	• Creativity and imagination • Dramatic play • Emotional expression • Self-image/self-awareness • Social interaction

What to Do:

1. Gather a collection of hats.

2. Stand in front of a mirror so your child can see himself.

3. Place the first hat on his head.

4. Let him admire himself in the mirror.

5. Then ask him to act like the person who might wear that sort of hat.

6. Join in the game by choosing a hat yourself and acting like that character.

7. Act out a drama together wearing the hats!

8. Exchange the hats for new ones and act out the new characters.

Variation: Add other dress-up items to go with the hats. Mix and match them for fun.

Caution: Be sure the articles of clothing are safe to wear, with no pins, sharp edges, and so on.

i CAN DO iT!

Help your child become aware of all the wonderful things she can do! This is a great way to build her self-confidence and self-esteem.

Materials:
- Magazines with pictures or picture books that show kids doing things

Learning Skills:	• Cognitive/thinking skills • Language and vocabulary development • Self-esteem/self-confidence • Social skills

What to Do:
1. Look through magazines or picture books together that show kids doing things.

2. Ask your child if she can do the things that are shown.

3. Have her explain how she does them.

4. Let her demonstrate if she likes!

5. If she says she can't do something, ask her why not.

6. Discuss with her all the things you can and cannot do. Make sure to explain how or why not.

Variation: Ask your child to try an activity she thinks she might be able to do but hasn't done yet such as pouring milk, tying her shoelaces, brushing her teeth, putting on her clothes, and so on. Help her as needed!

Caution: Make sure to select plenty of pictures of activities your child knows how to do, so she won't feel like a failure. Don't pressure her to do things she's not ready to do.

iLLUSTRATOR

Let your child draw his own pictures to illustrate a story!

Materials:
- Sheets of white paper
- Felt-tip pens or crayons
- Stapler
- Table

Learning Skills:	• Cognitive/thinking skills • Creativity and imagination • Emotional expression • Language and vocabulary development • Social interaction

What to Do:

1. Gather paper and felt-tip pens or crayons at a table.

2. Tell your child the first part of a story, making one up as you go.

3. When you reach an appropriate stopping point, ask him to draw a picture about what's happening.

4. When he finishes with the first picture, tell more of the story and have him continue to illustrate.

5. When you finish reading and your child finishes drawing, staple his illustrations together.

6. Go through his pictures one by one and write down the parts of the story under the appropriate illustrations.

Variation: Select a picture book and read the story to your child. As you read each page, have your child draw a picture to illustrate what's happening. When you finish the story, staple his illustrations together. Then read the picture book together and compare his illustrations with the book illustrations.

Caution: Be careful with the stapler around your child.

MAKE A MUMMY

Wrap your child in toilet paper and watch her transform into a scary monster!

Materials:
- Roll of toilet paper (preferably colored) or crepe paper
- Full-length mirror

Learning Skills:	• Creativity and imagination • Dramatic play • Emotional expression • Gross motor development • Self-image/self-awareness • Social interaction

What to Do:

1. Buy a pastel or printed roll of toilet paper, or use crepe paper if you like.

2. Have your child stand up straight.

3. Wrap her entire body with the paper, being careful not to cover her eyes, nose, or mouth. Wrap her arms and legs individually.

4. If the paper breaks off, just tuck in the loose end and continue.

5. When you finish, have your child face the mirror and see what she looks like. Don't forget to take a picture!

6. Have her walk around like a mummy, moving her arms and legs stiffly and slowly!

Variation: Let your child wrap you up with toilet paper!

Caution: Be sure not to cover your child's eyes, nose, or mouth, to avoid frightening her or causing breathing problems.

MIGHTY MEGAPHONE

Sometimes all it takes to inspire your child to use more words is something to talk into—like a Mighty Megaphone!

Materials:
- Paper-towel tube
- Stickers, printed contact paper, or felt-tip pens

Learning Skills:	• Cognitive/thinking skills • Creativity and imagination • Dramatic play • Emotional expression • Language and vocabulary development

What to Do:

1. Find an empty paper-towel tube.

2. Decorate the tube with stickers, contact paper, or felt-tip pens.

3. Show your child how to work the Mighty Megaphone by first talking without it, then using the megaphone.

4. Have him tell you stories using his megaphone!

Variation: Make two megaphones and enjoy a conversation with your child!

Caution: Tell your child not to run with the megaphone near his mouth, in case he trips and falls.

MY OWN ROOM

Your child develops part of her self-identity through her sense of her bedroom. Help her find out what's special about her room—and about herself!

Materials:
- Large sheet of paper
- Felt-tip pens
- Table

Learning Skills:	• Cognitive/thinking skills • Memory/mental imagery • Self-image/self-esteem • Spatial relationships

What to Do:

1. Place a large sheet of paper on a table.

2. Outline your child's bedroom on the paper, showing her where the door, window, closet, and bed are located.

3. Ask her what else is in her room.

4. Draw and label each item together as she lists the things in her room.

5. If she forgets some things, help her remember with clues.

6. When you finish, visit her bedroom and see how many things she remembered!

Variation: Have your child draw her room without your help. Also, encourage her to discuss the things in her room and why they are important to her.

Caution: Use nontoxic felt-tip pens.

PUDDING PAINT

You thought pudding was just for eating? Find out how much fun your child can have when he plays with pudding instead!

Materials:
- Smock
- Package of pudding mix or a container of ready-to-eat pudding
- Food coloring (optional)
- Large sheets of glossy paper or a clean tabletop
- Spoon

Learning Skills:	• Creativity and imagination • Emotional expression • Fine motor development • Sensory exploration

What to Do:

1. Cover your child with a smock to protect his clothes.

2. Mix the pudding—or remove the ready-to-eat pudding from its container—and place it in a bowl.

3. If you use vanilla pudding, mix in some food coloring for added fun.

4. Place some slick paper on a table, or use a clean tabletop.

5. Spoon some pudding onto the paper or tabletop.

6. Let your child fingerpaint with the pudding.

7. He can eat the leftovers when he's finished!

Variation: Use shaving cream or whipped cream instead of pudding for a different sensation.

Caution: If using shaving cream, be sure to tell your child not to put it in his mouth.

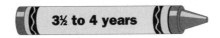

ROLLER BODY

With this fun activity, your child will develop increased body awareness and an enhanced sense of touch while enjoying a nice massage!

Materials:
- Clean rolling pin
- Washcloth
- Duct tape
- Blanket
- Carpeted floor

Learning Skills:	• Emotional expression • Self image/body awareness • Sensory stimulation • Social interaction

What to Do:

1. Cover a rolling pin with a washcloth and secure it with duct tape on the ends.

2. Lay a blanket over a carpeted floor.

3. Have your child lie on her tummy on the blanket and close her eyes.

4. Gently roll the rolling pin over her body while you sing a song. Make sure to roll over all her body parts.

5. When you finish with one side, roll her over and repeat.

Variation: When you finish with both sides, let your child roll the pin over you!

Caution: Roll the pin gently so the massage doesn't become unpleasant. Tell her to be careful handling the rolling pin, so she doesn't accidentally club you!

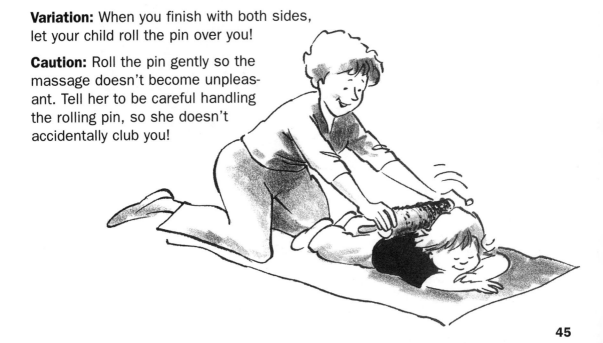

SAME AND DiFFERENT

Can your child tell how certain things are similar even though they're different? Play a game of Same and Different to find out!

Materials:
- Pictures of similar-looking people
- Pictures of animals, houses, foods, and other items that are similar yet different
- Floor or table

Learning Skills:	• Classification skills • Cognitive/thinking skills • Language and vocabulary development • Self-awareness • Social interaction

What to Do:

1. Select a variety of pictures from the categories above, including your own family members, if possible.

2. On the floor or table in front of your child, set out two pictures of similar looking people, houses, animals, and so on.

3. Ask him how the pictures are similar.

4. Ask him how they are different.

5. Provide clues if necessary.

6. Discuss his responses.

7. Repeat for the rest of the pictures.

Variation: Display your family members as a group and talk about how they are similar yet different. Talk specifically about how your child is similar yet different from other family members—and how that makes him special.

Caution: Be careful when comparing siblings, so your child doesn't feel inferior or jealous.

STEPPING STONES

It's fun to follow a path of stepping stones, even when the stones are really paper plates!

Materials:
- Paper plates
- Pen

Learning Skills:	• Body awareness • Cognitive/thinking skills • Gross motor development • Math/counting skills • Problem solving • Spatial awareness

What to Do:

1. Number the paper plates.

2. Place the plates in numerical order along a path through the house or yard. Separate them about the length of your child's step.

3. Make the path twist and turn, and choose interesting routes such as on a chair, over a pillow, under a table, and so on.

4. Have your child follow the paper plates in numerical order along the path.

5. Play again, creating a new path with the plates.

Variation: To make the game more challenging, space the plates farther apart. Have your child collect the plates as he follows the path.

Caution: Be careful where you lead your child, so she doesn't hurt herself trying to reach a plate.

TACKY TAPE

Sometimes all you need is a roll of tape to have fun together—and this roll of tape teaches your child all kinds of skills!

Materials:
- Roll of clear or colorful tape such as Scotch tape, masking tape, or electrical tape (Avoid duct tape.)

Learning Skills:	• Body awareness • Cause and effect • Eye-hand coordination • Fine motor development • Problem solving • Social interaction

What to Do:

1. Wrap a long length of tape around various parts of your body, sticking the tape to your clothes (and skin, if you like).

2. Greet your child and show him what you've done with the tape.

3. Ask him to help you remove the tape, offering him one end.

4. Have your child gently pull the tape from your body, turning and twisting as needed.

5. Repeat, this time covering your child with the tape. (Avoid his skin.)

6. Let your child pull the tape from his own body.

7. Play again, this time letting your child stick the tape to your body and remove it.

Variation: Stick the tape throughout the house and have your child follow the path, pulling the tape off as he goes.

Caution: Be careful not to stick the tape to your child's skin.

TALK LiKE ME

Can your child imitate your voice? Create several voices that imitate various characters, and have her try to copy the voices!

Materials:
- Pictures of different characters such as a man, woman, baby, animal, cartoon character, TV character, and so on

Learning Skills:	• Dramatic play • Emotional expression • Language and vocabulary development • Self-awareness • Social interaction

What to Do:

1. Collect pictures of different characters.

2. Show the first picture to your child.

3. Talk like the character using a creative and funny voice.

4. Have your child try to copy your voice and talk like the character, too!

5. Repeat for the other characters, changing your voice as you go.

Variation: Have your child make up the characters' voices.

Caution: Don't make your voices so loud that you hurt each other's ears!

HOWDY!

HOWDY!

TEA PARTY

Set up an afternoon tea party for your child and enjoy a special treat together!

Materials:
- Fruit-flavored herbal tea or juice
- Teapot and teacups
- Small table and chairs
- Tablecloth, china, and good silverware
- Teacakes, cookies, or small sand-wiches

Learning Skills:	• Dramatic play • Language and vocabulary development • Sensory awareness • Social interaction

What to Do:

1. Prepare the tea party by setting up a fancy table complete with your best dishes and tablecloth.

2. Make warm or cold tea or juice, and pour it into the teapot.

3. Sit at the table, pour tea, serve cookies, and chat.

4. Clean up together and plan another tea party for next week!

Variation: Have a special breakfast or lunch date.

Caution: Be sure the tea isn't too hot. If your child doesn't like tea, use juice or another favorite beverage.

TiCK, TOCK–FiND THE CLOCK

Your child has only a few minutes to find the ticking clock! Where can it be? She must listen carefully!

Materials:
• Timer or alarm clock that makes an audible ticking sound

Learning Skills:	• Cause and effect • Cognitive/thinking skills • Listening skills • Mental imagery • Problem solving

What to Do:

1. Hide a timer or alarm clock somewhere in the house or yard.

2. Have your child enter the area and listen carefully.

3. Tell your child she has three minutes to find the clock before the alarm goes off. She must listen carefully and follow the ticking sound of the clock!

4. Give her hints if she has trouble.

5. Play again, this time giving your child less time to find the clock.

Variation: Help your child find the clock by saying "hot" or "cold" as she moves closer to or farther from the target.

Caution: Don't hide the clock in an unsafe place, and make sure to reward your child's efforts!

WHATCHAMACALLiT!

Your child will enjoy making up names for unfamiliar, crazy-looking objects, and he'll have fun imagining what they do! The crazier, the better!

Materials:
- Several funny-looking objects unfamiliar to your child such as a garlic press, nose-hair plucker, beach shell, pizza cutter, hose nozzle, vacuum attachment, eyelash curler, and so on
- Paper bag

Learning Skills:	• Classification skills • Cognitive/thinking skills • Creativity and imagination • Language and vocabulary development • Social interaction

What to Do:

1. Place the items in a paper bag and set it between you and your child.

2. Have your child select one of the items.

3. Ask him to make up a funny name for the item.

4. Then have your child imagine what the item does and describe it for you.

5. Have him select the next item and repeat.

6. Continue playing until he names and describes all the items.

Variation: Instead of having your child describe what the item does, have him pantomime the item's function while you try to figure out what he means!

Caution: Be sure the items are safe to handle.

WHEELIE-STICK!

4 TO 4½ YEARS

The Fantastic Fours are particularly fun years! Your child is learning most of his skills through play. At this age, play is your child's equivalent of work. Play allows your child to use information in creative ways, relieve his frustrations, and enhance his development. Here are some important aspects of play:

- Your child is developing important social skills through interaction with other people—both real and imaginary. Expose him to friends and family and provide him with dolls, action figures, and stuffed animals, so he can learn to relate in different ways through make-believe, sharing, and role-playing.

- Through play, your child learns concepts that will provide the foundation for more complex learning. Each time he engages in play, he practices his thinking skills, uses his language skills, and solves problems. Encourage these building blocks of learning by providing interesting challenges through play.

- Your child's physical skills increase during play as he manipulates toys, plays with balls, builds with blocks, sifts in sand, and splashes in water. Make sure he has lots to enjoy.

- Your child has the opportunity to master life situations in the safe and controlled environment of play. Provide him with dress-up clothes, play utensils, doctor's kits, pencils and paper, and so on, to help him act out his interests, fears, and experiences.

BAKE A CRAZY CAKE

Cooking, which helps your child learn many important skills, is something you should do together as often as possible!

Materials:
- Yellow or white cake mix
- Mixing bowls
- Measuring and mixing spoons
- Character-shaped, round, or square cake pan
- Food coloring
- Colorful sprinkles
- Can of frosting
- Tubes of icing and other edible decorations (optional)
- Oven

Learning Skills:	• Cause and effect • Cognitive/thinking skills • Fine motor development • Math/counting skills • Scientific properties • Social interaction

What to Do:

1. Buy a yellow or white cake mix.

2. Help your child do the measuring, pouring, stirring, and mixing, following package directions.

3. Have your child add his favorite food coloring to the mixed batter.

4. Let him swirl the color to make a design, or mix the color with the batter if he prefers to have it blended.

5. Add colorful sprinkles and mix.

6. Pour the batter into a cake pan.

7. Bake according to package directions.

8. After the cake cools, help your child spread the frosting.

9. Add details using tubes of icing and other decorations, if you like.

10. Serve and eat!

Variation: Make cookies, brownies, and other fun things to eat!

Caution: Watch your child carefully around the oven and hot kitchen utensils.

BUILD A HOME

Help your child build her first home. All you need is a large cardboard box, some craft materials, and lots of imagination!

Materials:
- Large appliance box
- Scissors, X-acto knife
- Duct tape
- Felt-tip pens, poster paints, decals, stickers, fringe, self-adhesive felt squares, and other decorating materials

Learning Skills:	• Cognitive/thinking skills • Creativity and imagination • Gross and fine motor development • Self-esteem

What to Do:

1. Ask for a large box at a local appliance store, or find one that was saved after your family bought a new refrigerator, washer, or big-screen TV.

2. Make a door on one side of the box by cutting horizontally along the top, down one side, and along the bottom the same distance as the top. Crease the uncut side to allow the door to open and close.

3. Cut out windows using the same technique. You can cut all four sides, so the windows will be permanently open, or you can leave a side uncut to allow your child to open and close the window.

4. Use duct tape to secure holes, smooth rough edges, and strengthen the base.

5. Help your child decorate her house with felt-tip pens, stickers, decals, and other decorative items.

6. Have her furnish the house with small chairs, pillows, toys, and other household items—whatever she wants!

7. Let her play house!

Variation: Help your child make a school, hospital, fire station, or any other building. She can make a whole city!

Caution: Be extra careful with the X-acto knife around your child. Use nontoxic, child-safe felt-tip pens and paints.

CATCH AND CALL

This activity improves your child's coordination and other important skills.

Materials:
- Medium-sized rubber ball
- Large open space

What to Do:
1. Find a medium-sized ball that's easy for your child to catch.

2. Stand in a large open space, preferably outdoors, a few feet from each other.

Learning Skills:	• Cognitive/thinking skills • Eye-hand coordination • Fine and gross motor development • Language and vocabulary development • Reflexes • Social interaction

3. Think of a simple category such as toys or snacks.

4. Have your child think of examples from the category.

5. Begin tossing the ball back and forth.

6. As each person catches the ball, he must call out an example from the selected category.

7. If someone drops the ball, change categories and play again.

Variation: To make the game easier, sit on the floor with your legs apart and roll the ball back and forth, saying an example from the category each time you receive the ball.

Caution: Play in an open area so you don't break anything. Toss the ball gently.

ICE CREAM...

COOKIES...

CHALK CHARACTERS

Turn your child into a superhero, fairy princess, silly monster, and so on, with a little help from sidewalk chalk!

Materials:
- Colored sidewalk chalk
- Sidewalk or driveway
- Sunny day

Learning Skills:
- Cognitive/thinking skills
- Creativity and imagination
- Dramatic play
- Emotional expression
- Fine and gross motor development

What to Do:

1. Go outside on a sunny day with some sidewalk chalk.

2. Have your child stand on the sidewalk while you draw an outline around her shadow.

3. Let her add details to the outline using different-colored chalk.

4. Encourage her to create a fantastic character out of the outline such as a superhero, princess, monster, and so on.

5. Have her make as many chalk characters as she likes!

Variation: If the sun's not shining, have your child lie down on the sidewalk while you draw an outline of her body with the chalk.

Caution: Be sure the area is clear of broken glass or any other dangerous items.

DRESS-UP CLOTHES

Watch your child transform himself into a completely different person, just by putting on a few fancy outfits!

Materials:
- Dress-up clothes from a local thrift store such as dresses, skirts, and jumpers; pants, shirts, and belts; jackets, coats, and vests; shoes, hats, and wigs; gloves, jewelry, and scarves; fancy fabrics with sequins, feathers, fur, silk, chiffon, leather, and so on
- Large box

Learning Skills:	• Cognitive/thinking skills • Creativity and imagination • Dramatic play • Emotional expression • Fine and gross motor development

What to Do:

1. Buy a variety of dress-up clothes and put them in a large box.

2. Set the box in the center of the play area and let your child open it.

3. Have him explore the clothing and accessories and put together an outfit.

4. When he's dressed, ask him who he is and what he's going to do. Encourage him to act out his new identity.

5. Let your child wear the clothes for a while, then let him change into something new.

Variation: Have your child put on a one-person play with his dress-up clothes. Or, have him invite a friend over and have them act out a dramatic scene together.

Caution: Check the clothes for pins and other unsafe items before putting them in the box.

DRUM A CHANT

Can your child drum a chant-chant-chant? All it takes is a beat-beat-beat! Drum-a-chant, to-the-beat!

Materials:
• 2 drums or other objects to drum on

Learning Skills:
• Cognitive/thinking skills
• Coordination and rhythm
• Emotional expression
• Language and vocabulary development
• Social interaction

What to Do:

1. Find two drums, one for each of you, or make drums from oatmeal containers. You could also use a tabletop or other surface.

2. Tap a rhythm on the drum such as *tap-tap-tap*.

3. Have your child imitate the rhythm on her drum.

4. When she has the rhythm down, add words to go with the drumming. For example, as you drum *tap-tap-tap-tap*, you might say, "My name is Jane."

5. Continue to create drumming rhythms and chants, changing the rhythm and the words as often as you like. Have the other person follow the leader.

6. Take turns copying one another.

Variation: Have a "conversation" where one person speaks and the other person matches the words with a drumming rhythm. Take turns speaking and drumming.

Caution: Make sure your child doesn't drum too hard and hurt her fingers. If your child becomes confused, slow down the beat.

MY-NAME-IS-JANE...

EDIBLE PLAY DOUGH

Here's some play dough your child can play with, decorate, and then eat!

Materials:
- Homemade or packaged gingerbread dough
- Table
- Sprinkles and small candies
- Cookie cutters, rolling pin, plastic knife and fork, and other utensils
- Cookie sheet
- Oven

Learning Skills:	• Cause and effect • Creativity and imagination • Emotional expression • Fine motor development

What to Do:

1. Make gingerbread dough from a favorite recipe. Add extra flour if the dough is wet, until it has the consistency of play dough. Add water if it's too dry.

2. Set the dough on the table.

3. Have your child use various utensils to shape the dough into charactes, animals, and whatever he likes.

4. Let him decorate the shapes with sprinkles and small candies.

5. When he finishes, place the items on a cookie sheet and bake them according to package or recipe instructions.

6. Cool, serve, and eat!

Variation: Make gingerbread cookies, decorate with tubes of icing, and serve at snack time.

Caution: Be careful with your child around the hot oven, and make sure the dough utensils are safe to handle. If the dough contains raw eggs, make sure your child doesn't eat any.

FOOT FACE

Have your child make a crazy-looking sock puppet called Foot Face!

Materials:
- Clean sock
- Piece of cardboard
- Scissors
- Permanent felt-tip pens
- Yarn, buttons, and other decorative items (optional)
- Needle and thread (optional)

Learning Skills:	• Creativity and imagination • Emotional expression • Fine motor development • Language and vocabulary development • Self-image/self-esteem

What to Do:

1. Find a clean sock roughly your child's size.

2. Cut a piece of cardboard into a shape slightly larger than the sock.

3. Stretch the sock over the cardboard.

4. Have your child draw a crazy face near the toe end of the sock, using permanent felt-tip pens. Help her draw if necessary.

5. Draw the bottom of the mouth near the heel of the sock.

6. Draw a tongue and teeth in their appropriate locations.

7. Sew on yarn hair, button eyes, and other details, if you like.

8. Remove the sock from the cardboard and slip it onto your child's hand.

9. Let her make Foot Face come alive by opening and closing her hand while she talks for the puppet!

Variation: Make two sock puppets, one for each hand, and have your child put on a puppet show.

Caution: Supervise the use of the permanent felt-tip pens. If you sew on extra details, be sure they are secure.

MAGNET HUNT

Here's a different kind of treasure hunt full of scientific surprises! Let your child discover what items stick to the magnet!

Materials:
• Magnet appropriate for a child

Learning Skills:	• Classification skills • Cognitive/thinking skills • Gross and fine motor development • Scientific properties/exper-imentation

What to Do:

1. Buy or borrow a magnet appropriate for a child, available at toy and teacher supply stores. Find a magnet that is reasonably strong but not too powerful for your child to control.

2. Demonstrate how the magnet works on a few sample items.

3. Have your child walk around the house looking for things that might be magnetic.

4. After he's tested several objects, ask him to guess whether an item will stick to the magnet or not.

5. Have him continue his magnetic treasure hunt. Make sure to supervise any tests he wants to perform.

6. When he finishes, have your child talk about what items were magnetic and what those items have in common.

Variation: Collect a number of items from around the house and place them on a table. Ask your child to guess which ones are magnetic. Have him test the items and sort them into magnetic and nonmagnetic piles.

Caution: Be sure the items he tests are safe to touch.

MiGHTY BLOCKS

Help your child make her own blocks out of milk cartons. She can add to her collection every time a carton is emptied!

Materials:
- Milk cartons (pint, quart, and gallon)
- Scissors
- Pen or pencil
- Ruler
- Duct tape
- Decorative contact paper, stickers, or oil-based paint and paintbrushes

Learning Skills:
- Cause and effect
- Creativity and imagination
- Fine and gross motor development
- Problem solving

What to Do:
1. Cut off the tops of the milk cartons.

2. Rinse and dry the cartons.

3. Measure the width of the first carton along a bottom edge.

4. Measure and mark this same distance up from each bottom corner.

5. Cut downward from the top corners, stopping at each mark.

6. Fold the top flaps inward to make the carton a cube and tape with duct tape.

7. Cover the cube with decorative contact paper and stickers, or paint with oil-based paint.

8. Repeat with the other cartons. When the blocks are ready, let your child have fun stacking, building, and knocking them over!

Variation: Have your child help make the blocks for an added learning experience.

Caution: Be careful with the scissors and paint around your child.

MYSTERY BOX

Kids love a mystery. Create a mystery out of a simple box by hiding something mysterious inside!

Materials:
- Several items familiar to your child such as his shoe, toy, doll, special cup, favorite book, and so on
- Paper bag
- Small box such as a shoebox
- Tape

Learning Skills:	• Classification skills • Cognitive/thinking skills • Mental imagery • Problem solving • Social interaction

What to Do:

1. Collect several familiar items and place them in a paper bag so your child can't see them.

2. Tell your child to close his eyes, then remove one item from the bag and place it in the box.

3. Close the lid, tape the box shut, and give it to your child to hold.

4. Tell him there's something mysterious inside.

5. Let him feel the weight, shake the box, and think about it for a while.

6. Give him a clue about what's inside and let him guess what it is.

7. Continue giving clues until he guesses the item correctly.

8. Open the box, reveal the item, and play again!

RATTLE!

CLUNK!

Variation: Let your child take a turn hiding items inside the box for you to guess!

Caution: Be sure all items are safe to handle.

PICTURE STORY

It's fun to look at family photos to inspire precious memories. See if your child can put the photos in chronological order!

Materials:
- 3 or 4 photos of a family vacation, birthday party, or other special event in your child's life
- Table

Learning Skills:	• Classification skills
	• Cognitive/thinking skills
	• Fine motor development
	• Prereading skills
	• Sequencing/seriation
	• Social interaction

What to Do:

1. Mix the photos up and set them on a table.

2. Ask your child to try to remember what happened first and have her choose the appropriate photo.

3. Then have her select the photo that represents what happened next.

4. Continue until she selects all the photos and places them in chronological order.

5. Have her tell the story of what happened from beginning to end, asking questions to help her remember more details.

Variation: Take out several photos from various events and have her sort them according to event. Then have her put each event in chronological order.

Caution: Tell your child to handle the photos carefully, or have copies made for her to use.

PUZZLE PiCTURE

Your child will have as much fun creating his own puzzle as he has putting one together. Make sure you choose a picture that's interesting to him.

Materials:
- Interesting photo of a family member, favorite animal, cartoon character, and so on
- Poster board
- Spray adhesive
- Black felt-tip pen
- Scissors
- Small box
- Table

Learning Skills:	• Classification/sorting • Cognitive/thinking skills • Fine motor development • Mental imagery • Problem solving

What to Do:

1. Find an interesting picture.

2. Spray adhesive over the surface of the poster board.

3. Press the picture onto the sprayed surface and allow it to dry.

4. Use a black felt-tip pen to draw large, simple puzzle lines on the picture.

5. Cut out the picture along these lines to form puzzle pieces.

6. Place the pieces in a small box.

7. Sit at the table with your child and present him with the box.

8. Have him open the box, dump out the pieces, and put the puzzle together.

9. If he needs help, give him clues so he can put the puzzle together himself.

10. When the picture is complete, have him talk about what he sees.

Variation: Let him help you make the puzzle from the beginning, then have him put it together.

Caution: Be careful when using spray adhesive and scissors around your child, and make sure the room is well ventilated.

SCRATCH PiCTURE

Your child will enjoy watching her drawing magically appear in color as she draws on a black surface!

Materials:
- Sheet of poster board or stiff paper
- Scissors
- Variety of colored crayons
- Black poster paint and paintbrush
- Paper clip or turkey skewer

Learning Skills:	• Cause and effect
	• Creativity and imagination
	• Emotional expression
	• Fine motor development

What to Do:

1. Cut out a small square of poster board about 4 inches by 4 inches.

2. Have your child color the entire surface with different-colored crayons. Ask her to press hard as she colors.

3. Then have her paint over the entire picture with black poster paint. Allow the paint to dry completely.

4. Give your child an opened paper clip or a turkey skewer, and have her draw a picture by scratching a design over the black paint.

5. She'll be amazed as the design magically appears in color!

Variation: Use Crayola Changeable felt-tip markers for a different effect. Have your child use one marker to draw a design, then have her draw over the design with another marker to change it to a different color!

Caution: Teach your child how to use sharp instruments safely.

SHAPE SHiFT

At this age, your child has a flexible body that can twist into many different shapes. See how many shapes he can make!

Materials:
- Length of rope the size of your child, from his toes to his fingertips stretched over his head
- Scissors
- Floor space

Learning Skills:	• Cognitive/thinking skills
	• Gross motor development
	• Self-awareness
	• Spatial relationships

What to Do:

1. Measure and cut a length of rope the size of your fully extended child.

2. Clear the floor or lawn of obstacles.

3. Lay the rope down in a straight line and have your child lie down directly on top of it.

4. Twist the rope into a curve and have your child lie directly on top of it, making the same shape.

5. Change the rope design to create new shapes for your child to make such as an S curve, V shape, wiggly line, circle, triangle, square, and so on.

Variation: Have your child design the rope shapes and try to shift his body to make the shape. Or, write the letters of the alphabet with the rope and see if he can make all twenty-six letters!

Caution: Be sure the playing surface is clean and safe for him to lie on.

SHAPE WALK

Learning shapes will be fun for your child as you take her on a shape walk inside or outside the house!

Materials:
• Area with lots of shapes to see

What to Do:
1. Show your child the different shapes you want her to look for on your walk such as a circle, square, triangle, rectangle, oval, and so on.

Learning Skills:
• Body awareness
• Classification/sorting skills
• Cognitive/thinking skills
• Language and vocabulary development
• Social interaction
• Spatial relationship

2. Take a walk through the house, yard, park, or neighborhood.

3. Select one shape and have her see how many items she can find that have the same shape.

4. After she finds five or so, change to another shape and repeat.

5. Continue until she's looked for all the shapes.

6. When you finish, have a snack together and ask her what shape her cracker, cookie, or sandwich is!

Variation: Bring a pad of paper on your walk, and have your child draw the object each time she finds a shape.

Caution: Watch where you walk so she doesn't trip and fall while trying to spot all those shapes!

SHARE A SCUPTURE

Working together on a sculpture will be fun as you share your creative ideas while making a work of art.

Materials:
- Play dough, baker's clay, clay, or other sculpting material
- Table

Learning Skills:	• Cause and effect
	• Emotional expression
	• Fine motor development
	• Problem solving
	• Sharing and cooperation
	• Social interaction

What to Do:

1. Buy or make different-colored play dough or clay.

2. Divide the dough. Give one half to your child and keep the other half.

3. Begin the sculpture by shaping a small piece and setting in on a table.

4. Have your child shape a small piece and add it to your piece.

5. Work back and forth, creating new pieces to add to the sculpture. Watch it change as you work!

6. When you use all the dough, admire your piece of art and select a name for it together.

Variation: Have your child work on his own sculpture while you work on yours. After a few minutes, change seats. Have him work on your sculpture while you work on his. Continue until you both finish with the sculptures.

Caution: Be sure to use nontoxic sculpting material.

STOP 'N' GO DANCING

It's easy to listen to fun music and dance to the beat. But can your child stop suddenly when the music abruptly ends?

Materials:
- Cassette player
- Tape or CD with dance music

Learning Skills:	• Creativity and imagination • Emotional expression • Gross motor development • Listening skills • Self-awareness • Spatial relationships

What to Do:

1. Find a tape or CD with fun dance music.

2. Have your child stand in the middle of the room and wait for the music to begin.

3. When you push "play," have your child start to dance.

4. When you push "stop," she must stop dancing and remain perfectly still until the music starts again.

5. Continue playing and stopping until the song is over.

6. Repeat with another song or different type of music.

Variation: Every time your child stops dancing, have her do a different kind of dance when the music starts again. Or, let her take a turn stopping and starting a song while you dance!

Caution: Be sure the room is free of obstacles.

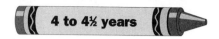
STRING A NECKLACE

Let your child make his own necklace with a few macaroni noodles and some string.

Materials:
- 8 bowls
- Food coloring (red, blue, green, and yellow)
- Small, straight macaroni noodles
- 4 stirring spoons
- Paper towels
- String
- Large, dull yarn needle

Learning Skills:	• Cause and effect • Cognitive/thinking skills • Creativity and imagination • Fine motor development • Self-awareness/self-esteem

What to Do:

1. Squeeze several drops of food coloring, one color per bowl, into four separate bowls.

2. Divide the noodles into four piles and pour them into the four bowls. Make sure to use macaroni that is straight, not curved.

3. Stir the noodles until they are all tinted.

4. Pour the noodles onto a paper towel to absorb the excess color.

5. Allow the noodles to dry, then place them in four separate bowls.

6. Give your child a length of string to make a necklace.

7. Tie one macaroni noodle to one end of the string.

8. Thread the large needle on the other end.

9. Let your child place macaroni noodles on the string, using the needle, until the string is full.

10. Tie the ends of the string together and place the necklace over his head.

Variation: Use colored cereals with holes in them instead of macaroni noodles.

Caution: Teach your child how to use the large needle carefully. Make sure the necklace is long enough to fit over your child's head.

STYLING SALON

Take your child to the Styling Salon—right in your own bathtub! Your child will get clean while she gets styled!

Materials:
- Bathtub
- Kids' shampoo
- Food coloring
- Hair clips
- Unbreakable mirror

	Learning Skills:	• Body awareness • Creativity and imagination • Emotional expression • Fine motor development

What to Do:

1. Fill the tub with warm water.

2. Have your child climb in.

3. Pour a small amount of shampoo into your hand—enough to make suds—and add a few drops of food coloring to tint (it rinses out easily).

4. Shampoo your child's hair, working up a good lather.

5. Hold up the mirror so your child can see herself.

6. Let her make different hairstyles with the colored shampoo.

7. Use clips and other hair holders for added fun.

8. Don't forget to take some pictures!

9. Rinse out the shampoo when finished.

Variation: Mousse your child's hair before putting her into the tub, then let her play with different hairstyles. Wash out the mousse with a normal shampooing.

Caution: Use baby shampoo to avoid stinging your child's eyes. Keep a washcloth handy to wipe away shampoo drips.

TABLE TALK

Here's a learning game you can play when you're at a restaurant waiting for your meal to arrive.

Materials:
- Several items placed on the table such as silverware, plates, salt and pepper shakers, napkin holders, toothpicks, sugar packets, syrup, menus, and so on

Learning Skills:	• Classification skills • Cognitive/thinking skills • Language and vocabulary development • Problem solving • Social interaction

What to Do:

1. While you wait for your meal at a restaurant, tell your child you're thinking of something that's sitting on the table.

2. Give him a clue such as the color, size, weight, function, and so on.

3. Let him try to guess what it is.

4. Cheer when he gets it right!

5. If he guesses incorrectly, continue providing clues.

6. After he guesses correctly, let him take a turn choosing an item and providing clues for you.

7. Take turns until you run out of items on the table.

Variation: Expand the game to include items around the restaurant.

Caution: Don't let your child wander away from the table. Tell him he must locate the item from his seat.

TAKE-A-TURN PiCTURE

Two heads are better than one when it comes to finishing a work of art.

Materials:
- 2 large sheets of paper
- Crayons or felt-tip pens
- Table
- Timer

Learning Skills:	• Cause and effect • Creativity and imagination • Fine motor development • Social interaction

What to Do:

1. Give your child one sheet of paper and keep one for yourself.

2. Sit opposite each other at a table and begin drawing a picture with the crayons or felt-tip pens.

3. Set the timer for one minute.

4. When the timer rings, switch your papers and continue drawing the other person's picture!

5. Reset the timer and repeat until the pictures are finished.

6. Name the pictures and hang them on the walls for show!

Variation: Both of you begin drawing a picture of an animal or person, starting with the head. When you finish the head, exchange papers and draw the bodies. Exchange again and draw the arms, legs, tails, and so on until the pictures are complete!

Caution: Use nontoxic felt-tip pens.

TELEPHONE TALK

Sometimes it's more fun to chat on the telephone than to talk face to face. You'll have fun making play cell phones and having a conversation with your child!

Materials:
- 2 small rectangular boxes long enough to fit from your child's ear to his mouth such as candy boxes
- Scissors
- Printed contact paper, spray paint, stickers, or other stick-on items

Learning Skills:	• Cognitive/thinking skills • Fine motor development • Language and vocabulary development • Social interaction

What to Do:

1. Make two cell phones by covering small, thin, rectangular boxes with colorful contact paper or spray painting them a bright color.

2. Cut out a hole at the top of one side for your ear, and a hole at the bottom of the same side for your mouth.

3. Give your child his cell phone and let him decorate it with stickers and other items.

4. Go across the room and call him on the cell phone, or have him call you.

5. Have a conversation about the day's events or whatever you like!

Variation: If you have real cell phones, you might use them instead of the play phones, but you don't have to turn them on.

Caution: Be sure all the rough edges are smoothed out.

TIPTOE, SNEAK, AND SNATCH

The excitement builds as your child tiptoes behind you and tries to snatch a toy!

Materials:
- Floor
- Toy or snack

Learning Skills:	• Body awareness • Cognitive/thinking skills • Fine and gross motor development • Problem solving • Social interaction • Spatial relationships

What to Do:

1. Sit on the floor in the middle of a room with your back facing the door.

2. Have your child wait in another room and count to ten.

3. Place a toy or snack behind your back.

4. When your child reaches ten, she must tiptoe into the room and try to grab the toy or snack before you catch her!

5. Take turns.

Variation: Wear a blindfold and place the item in front of you. Your child must tiptoe in and try to snatch the item. Reach out occasionally to try to grab her while she tries to retrieve the object!

Caution: Be sure the floor isn't slippery and don't swing your arms too hard in case you accidentally make contact with your child.

TUMBLING TOWER

Kids sometimes enjoy knocking things over more than they enjoy building them. Here's a fun building game with a surprise ending!

Materials:
- Uncarpeted floor or large table
- Blocks, crackers, or other stackable items

Learning Skills:	• Cause and effect • Fine motor development • Problem solving • Social interaction

What to Do:

1. Find a flat surface for the game such as an uncarpeted floor or large table.

2. Collect several stackable items such as blocks, crackers, or small flat toys.

3. Take turns stacking the items to build a tall tower.

4. Show your child how to be careful stacking the items as the tower grows taller and taller.

5. The player who makes the tower fall has to clean up the pieces!

6. Play again!

Variation: Instead of building a tower, create or buy a stacking game where you try to keep the tower from falling as you take turns removing pieces.

Caution: Make sure the items won't hurt your child if they fall.

4½ TO 5 YEARS

Dramatic play reaches its peak during the later preschool years. Your child is entering the creative world of make-believe, daydreaming, and fantasy play. You may find her talking to imaginary friends and acting out scenes from movies and TV. This vicarious play gives your child the opportunity to interact with peers in new ways, to explore situations that might be strange or frightening, and to assume various roles as she learns to be less egocentric. Here are the highlights of this dramatic period:

- Your child is expressing herself in healthy and creative ways as she tries out new roles. Help her dramatize a current interest, such as a favorite character, recent event, or familiar setting, and provide the accessories and props to make her interest come alive.

- Your child will especially enjoy the popular themes of dramatic play including housekeeping, going to work, taking care of dolls, setting up school, and acting out scary situations such as sickness and death. Provide your child with dress-up clothes so she can become a hero, monster, animal, ghost, and so on.

- Your child will need outdoor adventure time, too, as her flights of fantasy take her into the jungle, forest, or lava-filled volcano. Help her build forts, tents, and lean-tos so she'll have settings in which to dramatize her fantasies.

BALL IN THE BOWL

Here's a simple game that will be fun and challenging for your child.

Materials:
- Cleared floor area
- Small ball (not too bouncy)
- Large bowl

Learning Skills:	• Cause and effect • Cognitive/thinking skills • Fine and gross motor development • Problem solving • Spatial relationships

What to Do:

1. Clear the play area and place a bowl in the middle of the floor.

2. Seat your child a foot or two away from the bowl.

3. Give her the ball and tell her to toss it into the bowl. Demonstrate a few times if necessary.

4. After she makes a few shots, have her move a little farther back and try again.

Variation: Select several different-sized bowls or containers and place them in the middle of the room. Put stickers and other prizes in each bowl. When your child makes a shot, give her a prize from that bowl!

Caution: Avoid glass bowls. Use plastic or metal instead.

BUDDY BODY

Some say two heads are better than one. Are two bodies better than one? Find out while you have fun with your child!

Materials:
- Cleared floor area
- 2 rolls of cellophane or colored tape

What to Do:

1. Stand face to face with your child in the middle of a cleared area.

2. Give him one roll of tape and keep the other for yourself.

3. Tell him to begin taping himself to you while you tape yourself to him. Tape your arms, legs, stomachs, clothing, and so on!

4. Then figure out how to move across the room, working together!

5. Try to perform simple tasks like picking up toys, answering the phone, playing easy games, and so on.

6. Have scissors within easy reach if you need to free yourself quickly. Otherwise, try taking turns removing pieces of tape when you finish playing.

Variation: Tape stiff cardboard to your child's legs and arms, and have him walk like Frankenstein!

Caution: Play the game in a grassy or carpeted area, and try not to fall on top of your child.

Learning Skills:
- Cause and effect
- Cognitive/thinking skills
- Gross and fine motor development
- Problem solving
- Self-image/self-awareness
- Social interaction
- Spatial relationships

BUG HUNT

At this age, your child probably finds bugs fascinating! Have fun together on a Bug Hunt!

Materials:
- Pad of paper and felt-tip pens, or Polaroid camera
- Yard, park, nature walk, or other outdoor area
- Magnifying glass
- Bug identification book (optional)

Learning Skills:	• Classification skills • Cognitive/thinking skills • Respect for nature • Spatial relationships • Visual discrimination

What to Do:

1. Walk or drive to a park or nature area. Bring a small pad of paper and drawing materials, or a Polaroid camera, if you prefer.

2. Walk through the area and help your child find some bugs. Use a magnifying glass to get a closer look.

3. When you locate a bug, have your child draw a picture of it using her pad and pens, or take a photograph.

4. Continue your walk, looking for different bugs.

5. After you gather a nice collection, return home to organize the drawings or photos. If using a regular camera, have the film developed.

6. Lay the pictures or photos on a table and have your child examine the bugs. Ask her to look for features that are similar and different.

7. If you have a bug identification book, have your child try to identify the bugs and label them.

Variation: Play the game again, but this time go on a Plant Hunt to find different kids of flowers and plants.

Caution: Be careful with bugs that bite and sting!

FACE PAINTING

Your child is developing a strong sense of self, so give him something new to look at when he peers in the mirror!

Materials:
- Set of nontoxic face paints or crayons, available at craft or toy stores
- Table or floor
- Mirror

Learning Skills:	• Creativity and imagination • Dramatic play/self-expression • Fine motor development • Language and vocabulary development • Self-awareness/self-esteem

What to Do:

1. Set out face paints on the table or floor.

2. Place a mirror nearby so your child can watch himself work.

3. Let him paint his face using his imagination.

4. When he finishes, take pictures, visit the neighbors, or scare other family members!

5. Have him make up a story that goes with the new face. Have him act it out if he likes.

Variation: Paint your child's face without letting him see. He'll be surprised when he looks in the mirror! Ask him to tell you what's different about each face he paints.

Caution: Be sure to use gentle, nontoxic face paints that wash off easily.

FACES HAVE FEELINGS

Your child experiences a wide range of emotions, but she doesn't always know how to express them. Here's a game that will help.

Materials:
- Pictures of people expressing emotions from inexpensive picture books or magazines
- Scissors
- Floor or table

Learning Skills:
- Cognitive/thinking skills
- Emotional expression
- Language and vocabulary development
- Self-awareness
- Social interaction

What to Do:

1. Collect some pictures of children and adults expressing emotions with their faces.

2. Cut out the pictures and pile them in a stack.

3. Sit with your child on the floor or at a table, and place the pictures between you, facedown.

4. Turn over the first picture and show it to your child.

5. Ask her what she thinks the person is feeling. Help her with vocabulary words if she can't express herself.

6. Ask her to imitate the face in the picture.

7. Talk with her about expressing various emotions and why this is important.

Variation: Take turns selecting a picture from the pile without showing the other person. Imitate the face in the picture and have the other person try to guess the emotion.

Caution: Be careful with scissors if you're cutting pictures.

FOIL FUN

Children love to try to guess what things are, especially when the items are fun and familiar!

Materials:
- Several of your child's smaller toys such as an action figure, stuffed animal, ball, block, doll, and so on
- Aluminum foil
- Paper bag
- Table or floor

Learning Skills:	• Classification skills • Cognitive/thinking skills • Fine motor development • Mental imagery • Social interaction

What to Do:

1. Collect a variety of your child's smaller toys.

2. Wrap each item in aluminum foil.

3. Place the items in a paper bag and set it on a table or floor, between you and your child.

4. Ask your child to close his eyes.

5. Bring out one item and hand it to him.

6. Tell him to feel the item and try to guess what it is.

7. After he guesses, unwrap the item to see if he's right.

8. Repeat until all the items have been identified.

9. Let your child take a turn wrapping items for you to guess.

Variation: To make the game more challenging, use items that are similar such as stuffed animals. It should be harder for your child to distinguish the items.

Caution: Make sure the wrapped items are safe to handle.

FOLLOW THE LEADER

Take turns being the leader! The follower must imitate every movement the leader makes as you move through the house or yard.

Materials:
• Large space

What to Do:
1. Decide who will be the leader first.

Learning Skills:	• Body image • Cognitive/thinking skills • Gross motor development • Problem solving • Spatial awareness

2. The leader must move around the house or yard, any way she likes, and the other person must follow her movements exactly.

3. At regular intervals, have the other person take a turn being the leader.

Variation: Play music in the background to stimulate creative movement. Or, try playing the game in a neighborhood park or gym.

Caution: Be sure the area is safe so that neither person gets hurt while leading or following. Watch your child carefully so she doesn't try any dangerous moves.

GRASSHOPPERS AND BUTTERFLIES

Your child will learn to stay alert and listen for directions in this funny game.

Materials:
- Pictures of grasshoppers, butterflies, and other insects that move in an interesting way
- Cleared room

Learning Skills:	• Cause and effect • Classification skills • Cognitive/thinking skills • Listening/attention span • Problem solving • Social interaction

What to Do:

1. Gather pictures of insects from library books or nature magazines.

2. Talk about the different insects and how they move. Demonstrate if necessary.

3. Stand in the middle of a cleared room.

4. Call out the name of the first insect, like "Grasshopper!"

5. Both of you must imitate the insect's movements, in this case hopping around like a grasshopper.

6. After several seconds, the other person must call out another insect's name such as "Butterfly!"

7. Both of you must instantly change to the movement of a butterfly.

8. Take turns calling out insects from the pictures you see, and change to the new movements.

Variation: Look for other animals, like reptiles and mammals, and imitate their movements.

Caution: Be sure there is enough room to move around freely and safely.

iN MY PURSE

Kids are curious about what you have in your briefcase or purse, so open it up and show your child what's inside.

Materials:
- Items inside your purse or briefcase
- Floor or table

Learning Skills:	• Classification skills • Cognitive/thinking skills • Language and vocabulary development • Mental imagery/imagination • Social interaction

What to Do:
1. Remove any items that might be dangerous or inappropriate for your child to handle.

2. Sit on the floor or at a table with your purse or briefcase between you and your child.

3. Ask her what she thinks is inside the purse or briefcase.

4. Pull out each item as she names it such as your keys, wallet, tissues, and so on.

5. Ask her if she knows what the items are used for.

6. If she has trouble thinking of items, give her clues by telling her what each item does.

Variation: Have your child fill a bag or purse with items, then you guess what's inside. Ask her to provide clues if necessary.

Caution: Make sure to remove all dangerous and inappropriate items.

MAGIC WAND

Does your child know his body is magical? All he needs is a magic wand to show you what it can do!

Materials:
- Magic wand, made from a 1- to 2-foot dowel or stick, covered with bright ribbons or painted with a rainbow of colors

Learning Skills:	• Classification skills • Creativity and imagination • Gross and fine motor development • Language and vocabulary development • Self-image/self-awareness • Social interaction

What to Do:

1. Sit on chairs opposite each other.

2. Tell your child you have a magic wand that can make his body do magical things.

3. Touch your child's hand with the wand.

4. Ask him to demonstrate the magical things he can do with his hand such as wave, grasp, wiggle, open, close, stretch, point, play the piano, and so on.

5. Continue touching his other body parts with the magic wand, including his feet, arms, legs, torso, head, fingers, toes, lips, shoulders, knees, and so on.

Variation: Take turns with the wand, demonstrating what your body parts can do.

Caution: Be careful not to accidentally poke each other.

OBSTACLE COURSE

As kids learn to do new things with their bodies, they love to try new challenges. And they never seem to get tired of obstacle courses!

Materials:
- Large room filled with obstacles such as pillows and cushions, blankets and sheets, large cardboard boxes, chairs and tables, bowls, buckets, baskets, tires, inner tubes, hoops, ropes, soft toys and blocks

Learning Skills:
- Cause and effect
- Cognitive/thinking skills
- Gross motor development
- Problem solving
- Self-awareness
- Spatial relationships

What to Do:

1. Collect several items for your child to move over, under, around, and through.

2. Set up the items along a course.

3. Start your child at the beginning of the course, and tell her to try to make it all the way to the end.

4. Watch her meet the challenges along the way, and praise her as she accomplishes each task!

Variation: Let her set up an obstacle course for you!

Caution: Be sure your child can safely navigate all the items, and don't use anything sharp or breakable.

PAPER PLATE AND CUP CONSTRUCTION

Show your child how he can build things using just about any materials. Have him start with paper plates and cups and see what he comes up with!

Materials:
- Several paper plates in a variety of sizes and colors
- Several paper cups in a variety of sizes and colors
- Smooth floor or cleared table
- Tape or glue
- Popsicle sticks (optional)

Learning Skills:
- Cause and effect
- Cognitive/thinking skills
- Fine motor development
- Language and vocabulary development
- Problem solving

What to Do:

1. Place the paper plates and cups on a smooth floor or cleared table.

2. Ask your child to build something using the plates and cups.

3. Suggest ideas if he has trouble getting started, or show him how to stack the plates and cups in an alternating fashion.

4. Offer him tape or glue if he wants to connect the materials so they won't fall.

5. Offer other building materials to experiment with such as Popsicle sticks.

Variation: Work together on a cooperative building project.

Caution: Show him how to use the tape and glue properly and safely.

PiPE-CLEANER SCULPTURES

Try this fun activity to help your child enhance her manual dexterity.

Materials:
- Table
- Pipe cleaners in a variety of colors

Learning Skills:
- Cause and effect
- Cognitive/thinking skills
- Creativity and imagination
- Fine motor development
- Problem solving

What to Do:

1. Clear a table and have your child sit down to work.

2. Set the pipe cleaners on the table.

3. Show her how to use her fingers to bend, curl, twist, link, and shape the pipe cleaners.

4. Let her make whatever she wants. If she has trouble starting, suggest ideas such as animals, people, letters, numbers, buildings, freeform sculptures, and so on.

Variation: Work with your child on ambitious projects such as a zoo full of animals, a town full of buildings and people, an extended family, and so on.

Caution: Tell your child to be careful with the sharp points at the ends of the pipe cleaners.

SHOE SHOPPING

Walking is easy when the shoes fit. Why not have your child enjoy a wobbly walk with a fun game of shoe shopping!

Materials:
- Several types of adult shoes, including heels, boots, sandals, slippers, tennis shoes, and so on

Learning Skills:
- Cognitive/thinking skills
- Gross motor development
- Problem solving
- Self-image/self-awareness
- Spatial relationships

What to Do:

1. Gather a variety of shoes from your closets or buy some inexpensive ones from a thrift shop.

2. Display the shoes in a row so your child can "shop."

3. Let him pick out a pair of shoes and try them on.

4. Have him walk around the house, testing them out!

5. Ask him to perform some task while in the shoes such as stepping over a pillow or walking under a table.

6. When he finishes with one pair, have him pick out another and repeat.

Variation: Mismatch the shoes to make walking even more challenging.

Caution: Be sure the area is clear for walking, and don't include shoes that might lead him to twist his ankle. Watch him carefully during the wobble walk!

SiLLY WALKS

Now that your child knows everything about walking, challenge her with a game of Silly Walks!

Materials:
- Large play space

What to Do:

1. Find a large area so you have plenty of room to be creative.

Learning Skills:	• Cognitive/thinking skills
	• Creativity and imagination
	• Gross motor development
	• Self-expression/dramatic play
	• Social interaction

2. Start the game by having one person make up a silly walk such as rubber legs, one foot forward/one foot backwards, walk on your knees, walk with your legs wide apart, walk on your heels, walk toe-to-heel, and so on.

3. Take turns creating silly walks and have the other person copy the walk.

Variation: Think up other silly body movements besides silly walks. Encourage your child to be creative with her whole body!

Caution: Clear any obstacles that might pose a hazard.

SMELLY STUFF

Your child is becoming better at distinguishing smells as he learns more and more about his environment. He'll have fun with Smelly Stuff!

Materials:
- Several interesting items to smell such as a banana, cup of coffee, piece of fresh bread, flower, cologne, piece of rubber, teddy bear, and so on
- Paper bag
- Table or floor

Learning Skills:	• Classification skills • Cognitive/thinking skills • Mental imagery • Sense discrimination • Social interaction

What to Do:

1. Collect several odorous items and place them in separate paper bags.

2. Sit at a table or on the floor with the paper bags between you and your child.

3. Open one bag and hold it up to his nose, hiding the contents from view.

4. Ask him to guess what he smells.

5. Give him hints if he needs help.

6. When he guesses correctly, show him the item.

7. Repeat until all the bags are sniffed.

Variation: Select food items that have similar smells and see if your child can tell what's what.

Caution: Make sure the odors are not too strong.

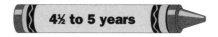
SOMEONE SPECIAL

Here's another fun guessing game for your child. Think of someone special and have her guess the person. It might even be her!

Materials:
- Pictures of family members, friends, famous people, and so on

Learning Skills:	• Classification skills • Cognitive/thinking skills • Language and vocabulary development • Mental imagery • Social interaction

What to Do:
1. Gather pictures of familiar people and set them on a table.

2. Have your child look over the pictures.

3. Tell her you're thinking of someone special. She must ask yes-or-no questions to find out who it is. Provide sample questions if necessary.

4. Have her ask questions until she guesses the special person.

5. Let her take a turn thinking of someone special, and have you ask yes or no questions.

Variation: To make it more challenging, remove the pictures from the table before she begins to ask questions.

Caution: Choose people familiar to your child so she doesn't become frustrated.

TEDDY BEAR PiCNiC

It's amazing how much your child learns with each activity—even at a Teddy Bear Picnic!

Materials:
- 1 or 2 teddy bears
- Sandwiches, drinks, cookies, and other treats
- Picnic basket
- Picnic blanket

Learning Skills:
- Cognitive/thinking skills
- Fine motor development
- Language and vocabulary development
- Self-expression/dramatic play
- Social interaction

What to Do:
1. Have your child find his teddy bears and tell them they're going on a picnic.

2. Prepare sandwiches, snacks, and drinks together.

3. Pack the food into a picnic basket. Be sure to include a picnic blanket.

4. Hike to the park with your teddy bears and basket, and find a nice picnic spot. Enjoy your lunch together while chatting about all sorts of things, and don't forget to include the bears in the conversation!

Variation: Instead of going to the park, have a picnic in the family room and pretend you're in the forest.

Caution: Teach your child to pack foods properly so they won't spoil in the outdoors.

TONGUE TALKER, TOE TAPPER

This activity requires some serious coordination—and that's the point. Your child can talk all she wants, but she must tap as she talks!

Materials:
- 2 pairs of shoes that make a sound when tapped on the floor, 1 for your child and 1 for you
- 2 chairs

Learning Skills:
- Coordination/body awareness
- Gross motor development
- Language and vocabulary development
- Social interaction

What to Do:

1. Have your child sit on a chair that allows her feet to reach the ground.

2. Put tapping shoes on her feet.

3. Put tapping shoes on your own feet and sit on a chair opposite her.

4. Choose a topic to discuss such as tomorrow's plans, what happened yesterday, or what you want to do on the weekend.

5. Take turns speaking. However, as you speak you must also tap each word. For example, if you say, "I want to go to the park," you must tap along with each word: tap-*tap*-tap-*tap*-tap-tap-*tap*. Encourage your child to tap louder on stressed syllables.

6. Continue the conversation until your tongues and toes get tired!

Variation: Put thimbles on your fingers and tap your words on the table!

Caution: Make sure your child can reach the floor with her feet so she doesn't fall off the chair trying to tap her words.

TOM THUMB

Encourage your child to dramatize human behavior while enjoying his funny fingers and thumbs!

Materials:
- Washable felt-tip pens in a variety of colors
- Small pieces of fabric
- Tape

Learning Skills:	• Cognitive/thinking skills • Dramatic play/imagination • Fine motor development • Language and vocabulary development • Social skills

What to Do:

1. Using your child's fingernails as faces, draw eyes, ears, hair, a nose, and a mouth on each finger and thumb using washable felt-tip pens. Draw members of your family, your child's friends, or other important people in your child's life.

2. Cut out small pieces of fabric large enough to wrap around your child's fingers and thumbs. Leave the nails exposed.

3. Tape the pieces of fabric to his fingers and thumbs. Try to have the outfits match the faces.

4. Encourage your child to act out a Tom Thumb play using his fingers as the actors! Help him get started if necessary.

Variation: Cut the fingers off old knitted gloves. Draw designs on the glove fingers with felt-tip pens and slip them onto your child's fingers. Have him act out another play!

Caution: Be sure the pens are washable and nontoxic.

TONGUE TWISTERS

Your child will have fun with tongue twisters at a time when her language skills are exploding!

Materials:
• Book of simple tongue twisters

What to Do:
1. Go to a library or bookstore and find a book of simple tongue twisters that suits your child's language level.

Learning Skills:	• Cognitive/thinking skills • Coordination • Language and vocabulary development • Listening skills • Problem solving

2. Read one of the tongue twisters several times, speaking slowly. You might try "A noisy noise annoys an oyster" or "She sells seashells down by the seashore."

3. Have your child try to say it with you.

4. Then have her try to say it by herself. Encourage her to say the whole thing without making any mistakes.

5. Laugh with her if she makes funny mistakes. It's all in fun!

Variation: Work together to make up your own tongue twisters.

Caution: Select manageable twisters so your child doesn't become frustrated or upset.

A NOISY NOISY NOISY WHAT?

TOY TALE

Here's a fun way to create a story: Each time you select a new toy, the story changes!

Materials:
- 6 to 10 of your child's toys such as a ball, doll, block, action figure, Lego piece, puzzle, paintbrush, car, and so on
- Paper bag
- Floor or table

Learning Skills:	• Cognitive/thinking skills • Creativity and imagination • Language and vocabulary development • Social interaction

What to Do:

1. Place the toys in a paper bag so your child can't see them.

2. Sit on the floor or at a table with the bag between you and your child.

3. Pull out a toy and begin telling a story featuring that toy. For example, if you pull out a ball, you might start your story by saying, "Once upon a time, there was a ball that bounced so high, it reached the sky!"

4. Pull out another toy and have your child continue telling the story featuring the new toy. For example, he might pull out a block and say, "The ball bounced to the ground and met a block who said, 'I wish I could bounce like you!'"

5. Continue taking turns pulling out toys and changing the story to fit the toys.

6. End the story with the last toy.

Variation: Play the same game with various categories of things such as food items, articles of clothing, stuffed animals, and so on.

Caution: Be sure the items are safe to handle.

WATER MUSIC

If your child thinks water is only for drinking and bathing, show her how much fun it can be to make water music!

Materials:
- 6 to 8 identical glasses
- Table
- Pitcher of water
- Food coloring (optional)
- Metal spoon

Learning Skills:	• Cause and effect
	• Classification skills
	• Cognitive/thinking skills
	• Creativity
	• Fine motor development
	• Listening skills
	• Problem solving

What to Do:

1. Set the glasses on a table.

2. Pour approximately one inch of water into the first glass.

3. Add water to the other glasses, increasing the amount by approximately half an inch each time.

4. If you like, add drops of food coloring to each glass, for more fun.

5. Have your child gently tap the first glass with a metal spoon.

6. Have her tap the next glass and ask her if the sound changed.

7. Have her tap the other glasses and listen to how the sound changes.

8. Ask her, "What seems to be happening?" Have her test her theory.

Variation: Have your child close her eyes and listen carefully as you tap a glass. Then tap another glass and ask her whether the note is higher or lower. Or, let her play a tune by gently tapping the spoon on different glasses.

Caution: Make sure your child taps softly on the glasses so they don't break.

WHAT CAN YOU DO?

Have your child use his imagination to think of fun things to do with various items!

Materials:
- Several items your child can use for creative thinking such as a long scarf, cardboard box, balloon, stick, towel, block, cup, and so on
- Paper bag

Learning Skills:	• Cognitive/thinking skills • Creativity and imagination • Mental imagery • Problem solving • Self-awareness/self-image

What to Do:

1. Place the items in a paper bag.

2. Select an item and ask your child to think of different things he can do with it. For example, if the item is a scarf, he might wave it, wrap it around his head, make a sling, wear it as a cape, tie it in a knot, make it into a necklace, roll it, fold it, wad it up and throw it, and so on.

3. Tally each function he thinks of. When he's finished, count how many uses he imagined!

4. Repeat with the other items.

Variation: Combine two items and ask him to imagine ways in which the items work together.

Caution: Make sure the items are safe to handle.

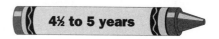

WHAT'S DIFFERENT ABOUT ME?

Your child looks at you every day, but does she really see you? Find out by playing this game!

Materials:
- Several different articles of clothing, pieces of jewelry, clothing accessories, and so on
- Floor

Learning Skills:	• Cognitive/thinking skills • Language and vocabulary development • Mental imagery • Problem solving • Social interaction • Visual discrimination

What to Do:

1. Sit with your child on the floor so she can see you clearly.

2. Ask her what you're wearing and help her describe your various articles of clothing and accessories.

3. Tell her to close her eyes.

4. Remove or change one article of clothing or accessory such as unbuttoning a sweater, placing your watch on your other arm, removing a necklace, turning your socks inside out, and so on.

5. Have her open her eyes and guess what's different about you.

6. Let her take a turn changing her look, while you guess what's different about her!

Variation: Place a pile of extra clothes in the middle of the room. When your child closes her eyes, exchange one item you're wearing for a similar item from the pile. See if she can tell what's different about you!

Caution: Make sure the articles of clothing and jewelry are safe for her to handle.

5 TO 5½ YEARS

The Fearless Fives offer your child more opportunities to enhance his independence. He is becoming increasingly autonomous as he initiates projects, works on his own tasks, increases his self-help skills, and generally does things by himself. Developing a sense of competence helps your child feel like a strong and confident person, which leads to higher levels of self-esteem. In return, good self-esteem fosters continued feelings of competence. Here are some ways to encourage his independence:

- Your child will feel a sense of pride and accomplishment when he learns to master skills such as tying his shoes, riding a bike, and brushing his teeth. You can help increase his self-esteem by providing fun tasks that challenge him without frustrating him. Just make a game of it!

- Your child is preparing for school by learning to be more independent. As his first teacher, you can play games that help improve his ability to follow directions, communicate needs, and have fun learning new things.

- Your child is beginning to enjoy the beauty of words on the page. You can help him prepare for reading by reading to him, telling him stories, talking with him often, and listening—really listening—to what he has to say.

A B C DAY

Your child will have fun learning his ABCs with this game that makes them come alive!

Materials:
• Room, yard, or store filled with easily identifiable things

Learning Skills:
• Classification skills
• Cognitive/thinking skills
• Language and vocabulary development
• Prereading skills
• Social interaction

What to Do:

1. Have your child choose one letter of the alphabet each day for twenty-six days. The letters don't have to be selected in any order.

2. Tell him the sound the letter makes, and give him some examples. If he chooses the letter T, make the T sound, then say, "truck," "town," "toys," "tiger," "teacher," and so on.

3. After your child practices the sound, go through the house, yard, or store and have him find as many things as he can that start with the letter T. For example, in your house he might find a toaster, train, table, teacup, teaspoon, and so on.

4. Spend the day looking for items that begin with the day's letter. The next day, have your child choose a new letter.

Variation: Write down the day's letter on a pad of paper and have him draw a picture of each item he finds that begins with the letter.

Caution: Help him avoid becoming frustrated by giving him hints and repeating the sound as he hunts for examples.

ADD A MOVE

Enhance your child's memory skills while she practices body skills with this fun-to-do game!

Materials:
- Large open space

What to Do:

1. Find a large open space in which to play the game.

2. Stand in the middle of the space, facing each other.

3. Start by moving one part of your body. For example, raise your arm.

4. Have your child imitate the movement.

5. Add a second movement to the first. Your child must imitate both movements in the order in which they were performed.

6. Add more movements until she can't remember what to do!

7. Have your child take a turn creating a series of body movements that you must imitate. Have her begin with one move and add a move until someone forgets.

Variation: Play the game with words instead of body movements.

Caution: Be sure the area is clear so you don't bump into anything.

Learning Skills:	• Body awareness/self-image • Cognitive/memory skills • Creativity and imagination • Emotional expression • Fine and gross motor development

ALL iN A ROW

Teaching your child how to organize things in a series helps him organize his world.

Materials:
- Items that can be arranged in a series:
  - Broken crayons, from smallest to largest
  - Buttons, from smallest to largest
  - Sticks, from shortest to longest
  - Cans, from smallest to largest
  - Colored items, from darkest to lightest
  - Toys, from smallest to largest
  - Dolls, from oldest to newest
  - Clothing, from softest to stiffest
- Floor or table

Learning Skills:	• Cause and effect • Cognitive/thinking skills • Fine motor development • Language and vocabulary development • Problem solving • Social interaction

What to Do:

1. Gather several items that can be organized in a series.

2. Place them in a pile in the middle of the floor or table.

3. Sit opposite your child with the pile between you.

4. Explain how the items could be organized, from shortest to tallest, smallest to largest, darkest to lightest, or whatever seems appropriate.

5. Ask him to organize the items by lining them up in a row.

6. If he has trouble, review the organizing principle and help him choose which item goes next.

7. Gather a new group of items and repeat.

Variation: Instead of having your child arrange the items in a series, have him classify them into groups according to some other organizing principle.

Caution: Be sure the items are safe to handle.

BACKWARDS DAY

Your child now understands how to do many complicated things. She'll have fun trying to do them backwards!

Materials:
- Some activity that can be done backwards such as eating lunch, putting on clothes, taking a walk, and so on

Learning Skills:
- Cause and effect
- Cognitive/thinking skills
- Fine and gross motor development
- Problem solving
- Self-awareness
- Social interaction

What to Do:
1. Choose a familiar activity that your child can do backwards.

2. Tell her it's Backwards Day, so she has to do things backwards.

3. Have her get dressed, eat lunch, take a walk, and so on—backwards!

Variation: Play Opposite Day, where you say one thing but mean the opposite!

Caution: Be sure the activities are safe for your child to do backwards.

BALLOON BLOW

Balloons are wonderful toys that your child can play with in many different ways, and he learns while he plays!

Materials:
- 2 balloons
- Cleared floor or table

What to Do:

1. Blow up two balloons, one for each of you.

2. Place the balloons on the floor at one end of the room or yard.

Learning Skills:	• Cause and effect • Cognitive/thinking skills • Emotional expression • Fine and gross motor development • Problem solving • Social interaction • Spatial relationships

3. Get down on your hands and knees behind the balloons.

4. Start blowing your balloon to the other side of the room!

5. Whoever reaches the other end first gets to pick the next balloon event such as kicking the balloon, bouncing the balloon, kneeing the balloon, elbowing the balloon, head-butting the balloon, and so on.

Variation: Have a balloon relay race. Blow up several balloons and place the first on a plastic plate. Walk or run around the room without letting the balloon to fall off the plate! Take the next balloon and repeat until you've raced all the balloons.

Caution: Make sure not to overinflate the balloons, so they don't pop easily. Make sure you have a clear space to play in.

BOWLING BOXES

Help your child develop her all-important bowling arm with an easy game of Bowling Boxes!

Materials:
- 6 to 8 empty cereal boxes
- Tape
- Uncarpeted floor
- Medium-sized rubber ball

Learning Skills:	• Cause and effect
	• Cognitive/thinking skills
	• Fine and gross motor development
	• Self-awareness
	• Spatial relationships

What to Do:

1. Collect several cereal boxes and seal the tops with tape.

2. Set the boxes up in a triangle, like bowling pins, at one end of an uncarpeted room.

3. Have your child stand at the opposite end and give her the ball.

4. Have her roll the ball toward the cereal boxes and try to knock them down.

5. Roll the ball back to her and have her keep trying until all the boxes have been knocked down.

6. Set the boxes up again and play until she becomes tired of the game.

Variation: Have your child stand farther back each time she starts a new game. Or, set the boxes up like standing dominoes so that when she hits the first one, the others tumble down.

Caution: Make sure she's close enough to the boxes the first time so she doesn't become frustrated, and move all breakable items out of the way.

CLOUD CREATURES

You'll need a cloudy day for this game. Watch out for those big puffy Cloud Creatures!

Materials:
- Clouds
- Blanket

Learning Skills:
- Cognitive/thinking skills
- Creativity and imagination
- Emotional expression
- Language and vocabulary development
- Social interaction

What to Do:

1. Take a blanket outside on a cloudy day and spread it on the grass.

2. Lie down next to each other and look up at the clouds.

3. Ask your child what he sees in the clouds.

4. Tell him what you see.

5. Take turns making up stories that dramatize what you see in the clouds.

Variation: Have your child draw clouds that look like the cloud creatures. Have him make up stories to go with them.

Caution: Bundle up if it's cold and wear protective eye gear if necessary. Make sure you don't look directly into the sun!

DANCE A PART

It's easy for your child to dance when she uses her whole body, but what happens if she can only use one body part?

Materials:
- Cassette or CD player
- Dance music CD or cassette

Learning Skills:
- Cause and effect
- Cognitive/thinking skills
- Emotional expression
- Fine and gross motor development
- Problem solving
- Self-awareness/body image
- Social interaction

What to Do:
1. Find some dance music and place it in the cassette or CD player.

2. Switch on the music and listen to the rhythm.

3. Tell your child she can dance to the music, but she has to use only one body part at a time!

4. Select the body part such as her finger, hand, knee, face, shoulder, leg, toe, and so on. Have her move only that body part to the music.

5. Touch different body parts throughout the song and have her keep changing her dance.

Variation: Dance together and take turns calling out body parts to move.

Caution: Make sure the area is clear so you don't bump into anything.

DESIGN A LINE

Your child's artistic skills have greatly improved during the preschool years. It's time for him to show off his creativity with Design a Line!

Materials:
- Table
- Large sheets of white drawing paper
- Felt-tip pens

Learning Skills:	• Cognitive/thinking skills • Creativity and imagination • Emotional expression • Fine motor development • Social interaction

What to Do:

1. Sit at the table with your child.

2. Place a sheet of paper and some felt-tip pens in front of him.

3. Using one of the pens, make a wavy, straight, crooked, bending, or angular line on the paper.

4. Ask him to examine the design you made.

5. Then ask him to transform the design into a picture, using his imagination.

6. When the picture is finished, save it and play again!

Variation: Draw shapes instead of lines and see if your child can create a picture from your drawing.

Caution: Use nontoxic felt-tip pens.

FREEZE AND FLEE

How quickly can your child stop her body movements, then make them go fast again? Find out with Freeze and Flee!

Materials:
- Large area

What to Do:
1. Find a large space to play in, so your child can run around safely.

Learning Skills:	• Body awareness
	• Cognitive/thinking skills
	• Gross motor development
	• Listening skills
	• Social interaction

2. When you call "Flee!" your child must run around as fast as she can.

3. When you call "Freeze!" she must stop immediately and remain perfectly still.

4. Keep calling "Flee!" and "Freeze!" until she's tired.

Variation: Call out other commands such as "Jump!" "Dance!" "Walk!" "Crawl!" and so on.

Caution: Make sure the area is clear so your child won't bump into anything while running around.

GREETING CARDS

Help your child learn to express his feelings and recognize the feelings of others.

Materials:
- Colored construction paper
- Felt-tip pens
- Envelopes

Learning Skills:
- Cognitive/thinking skills
- Emotional expression
- Language and vocabulary development
- Self-awareness
- Social interaction

What to Do:

1. Talk with your child about a family member or friend who is celebrating a birthday, recovering from an illness, moving to a new home, and so on.

2. Fold a sheet of construction paper into quarters to form a card.

3. On the front, have your child draw a picture expressing an emotion related to the event. For example, if someone is sick, he might draw a picture of someone in bed with a thermometer in his mouth.

4. Inside the card, write down what he wants to say to the person such as "Get well soon" or "I miss you."

5. Place the card in an envelope and mail it.

Variation: Encourage your child to send cards without being prompted by a special occasion. He can send messages such as "I like you" or "You're the greatest!"

Caution: Help your child come up with the right words to convey the desired emotion.

iF i WERE . . .

What would your child do if she were something else? Find out with this fun game!

Materials:
- Magazines or inexpensive picture books
- Scissors

Learning Skills:	• Cognitive/thinking skills • Creativity and imagination • Emotional expression • Language and vocabulary development • Self-awareness/self-image • Social interaction

What to Do:

1. Cut out pictures of various animals, creatures, objects, places, and other items that will stimulate your child's imagination.

2. Arrange the pictures upside down in a stack.

3. Ask her, "What would you do if you were a . . .?"

4. Have her turn over the first picture and finish the sentence.

5. Then have her describe what she would do if she were the thing represented in the picture. Have her act out the role if she likes!

6. Continue playing with the rest of the pictures.

7. For fun, take a turn or two yourself!

Variation: Instead of using pictures of things, set up situations for her to imagine such as, "What would you do if you were lost? Or felt sick? Or saw a fire? Or found a dollar?" and so on.

Caution: Don't make the situations too scary.

MAGIC PICTURE

Watch your child's eyes light up as he makes magic pictures appear!

Materials:
- Sheets of white paper, medium thickness
- Crayons
- Flat items with raised designs that will show through the paper when rubbed with a crayon such as a leaf, doily, credit card, etched picture, stencil, thin necklace, coin, and so on
- Paper bag
- Table

Learning Skills:	• Cause and effect • Cognitive/thinking skills • Emotional expression • Fine motor development • Language and vocabulary development • Social interaction

What to Do:

1. Collect items your child can rub to create a design.

2. Place them in a paper bag so he can't see them.

3. Sit at the table with the bag, several sheets of white paper, and crayons.

4. Tell your child to close his eyes while you slip an item under the first sheet of paper.

5. Have him select a crayon and rub the paper until the magic picture appears!

6. Let him guess the item, then remove the paper to see if he's right.

7. Repeat for the rest of the items.

Variation: Have your child walk around the house looking for items that could make magic pictures. Have him try each one, then talk about why some work and others don't.

Caution: Use items that are safe to handle, and use larger crayons for easier manipulation.

PiCKUP FUN

By this age, your child knows very well how to grasp and release things with her hands. But can she pick up things using tongs?

Materials:
- Small items to pick up such as a piece of paper, small toy, cracker, pea, necklace, sandwich, and so on
- Floor or table
- Tongs
- Large bowl

Learning Skills:	• Cognitive/thinking skills • Coordination • Fine and gross motor development • Problem solving • Social interaction

What to Do:

1. Collect several small items that will be challenging but not impossible for your child to pick up with tongs.

2. Sit opposite her on the floor or at a table, and set the items between you.

3. Arrange them from easiest to hardest to pick up.

4. Set the bowl to one side, within reach of your child.

5. Give her a pair of tongs and let her try them out.

6. Have her try to pick up the first item with the tongs and place it in the bowl.

7. Have her continue picking up items until she has placed them all in the bowl.

Variation: Instead of using tongs, have your child use her toes to pick up items!

Caution: Make sure the tongs are easy to grip and don't have sharp teeth.

POUND, PINCH, AND PLAY

Play dough offers new challenges to kids at every level of development. Here are some suggestions for the preschooler.

Materials:
- Play dough, baker's clay, or other doughlike substance
- Kitchen utensils such as a large spoon, fork, dull knife, small bowl, garlic press, skewer, cookie cutter, cup, and so on
- Table

Learning Skills:	• Cognitive/thinking skills • Creativity and imagination • Emotional expression • Fine and gross motor development

What to Do:

1. Make or buy some play dough or baker's clay.

2. Set the dough and kitchen utensils on a table.

3. Let your child use the utensils to create whatever he wants with the dough.

4. If he has trouble getting started, suggest ideas for him to work on such as foods, animals, people, clothing, toys, and so on.

Variation: When your child finishes, bake the dough at 250°F for two to three hours to firm it up, then let him paint his creation.

Caution: Show your child how to use the utensils safely.

REARRANGE THE BEDROOM

Rearrange your child's bedroom and see if she can tell what's different!

Materials:
• Your child's bedroom

What to Do:
1. Have your child take a close look at her room.
2. Then have her leave the room and close the door.

Learning Skills:	• Cognitive/thinking skills • Language and vocabulary development • Self-awareness/self-esteem • Social interaction • Visual discrimination/scanning

3. While she's gone, change or remove a few items such as placing a pillow on top of the spread, turning her clock upside down, hanging her shoes where her jacket is supposed to be, and so on.

4. Have her reenter the room and take a look around.

5. Ask her if she can tell what's different about her room.

6. After she identifies all the changes, let her take a turn rearranging her room for you!

Variation: Go to a different room in the house and play again.

Caution: Make sure she avoids potentially dangerous objects when it's her turn to rearrange the room.

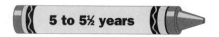

SECRET PiCTURE

Your child probably loves drawing pictures, so he'll really enjoy discovering secret drawings in your artwork!

Materials:
- White crayon and box of multicolored crayons
- Sheets of white paper

Learning Skills:	• Cognitive/thinking skills • Emotional expression • Fine motor development • Mental imagery • Social interaction

What to Do:

1. Draw a picture with white crayon on a sheet of white paper. Don't let your child see what you've drawn.

2. Have him sit at a table and place the paper in front of him.

3. Give him the box of crayons and tell him there's a secret picture on the paper.

4. He must figure out how to reveal the picture by coloring over the paper with the colored crayons. The white crayon drawing will resist the colors from the other crayons and reveal the secret picture. Provide hints if necessary.

5. Let him draw a secret picture for you!

Variation: Use Crayola Changeable felt-tip markers that include an invisible marking pen along with several colored pens that reveal the invisible markings.

Caution: Use small sheets of paper so your child doesn't get tired of coloring over large sheets.

SHADOW TAG

Here's a fun twist on the game of tag: Tag the shadow instead of the person!

Materials:
• Sunny outdoors

Learning Skills:	• Cognitive/thinking skills • Gross motor development • Self-awareness/self-image • Social interaction • Spatial relationships

What to Do:

1. Go outside on a sunny day and find your shadows.

2. Once you've found your shadows, run around trying to step on the other person's shadow while you try to avoid her stepping on yours.

3. Whenever someone's shadow is stepped on, she's it!

Variation: Stand so that your shadow hits a wall. Give your child a ball and have her try to hit your shadow with the ball. Keep moving so it isn't too easy!

Caution: Make sure the area is clear so your child doesn't bump into anything.

SHOW YOUR FEELINGS

Sometimes children have difficulty expressing their feelings appropriately. Here's a way to help your child learn to become more aware of his feelings and express them properly.

Materials:
- Pictures from magazines or inexpensive picture books showing people expressing emotions such as someone crying, laughing, angry, frightened, and so on
- Scissors

Learning Skills:	• Body awareness • Cognitive/thinking skills • Emotional expression • Gross motor development • Social interaction

What to Do:

1. Cut out pictures of people expressing emotions.

2. Discuss with your child what the people are feeling and explain how they are expressing their feelings.

3. Stack the pictures facedown in a pile.

4. Close your eyes while your child turns over the top picture.

5. Have him act out the emotion without using words.

6. You have to guess the emotion that he's trying to express.

7. After you guess correctly, switch places.

8. Take turns turning over pictures and acting out emotions.

Variation: Try acting out emotions with just your hands!

Caution: Select emotions that are appropriate for your child's level of development.

SORT THE SAME

Learning how to classify things is an important part of your child's cognitive development. Give her lots of opportunities to sort and separate.

Materials:
- Cupcake tin or egg carton
- Table
- 6 to 8 groups of small items to sort such as buttons, cereals, beads, beans, coins, raisins, and so on

Learning Skills:	• Classification skills • Cognitive/thinking skills • Language and vocabulary development • Math/counting skills • Problem solving

What to Do:

1. Set the tin or carton on a table.

2. Place the small items in a pile next to the tin or carton.

3. Have your child sit at the table near the materials.

4. Have her pick out one item and place it in one of the cups.

5. Have her select another item and decide whether the item belongs with the first item or needs its own cup.

6. Talk with her about how the items are similar and different.

7. Have her continue sorting the rest of the items.

8. Have her count the items in each cup to see which one has the most items.

Variation: Each time you take your child to the grocery store, sort the food items into groups such as cold, hot, meat, vegetables, boxes, bags, snacks, health food, and so on. Talk to her about how the items are similar and different.

Caution: Make sure your child doesn't swallow any of the nonedible small items.

STORYBOOK THEATER

Give your child the opportunity to act out his storybooks for you!

Materials:
- Favorite picture books
- Towel or sheet
- Floor
- Chair

Learning Skills:
- Cognitive/thinking skills
- Creativity/dramatic play
- Emotional expression
- Gross motor development
- Language and vocabulary development
- Self-awareness/self-esteem

What to Do:
1. Have your child select a few of his favorite picture books that he would like to act out.

2. Spread a large towel or sheet over the floor for the stage.

3. Sit in a chair and begin to read the story slowly.

4. Have your child stand in the middle of the stage and act out each scene as you read it.

Variation: Videotape the presentation, then play it back for him to watch!

Caution: Make sure none of the scenes is dangerous to act out. Read slowly and provide tips to get your child started, if necessary.

THREE THINGS

Some people say good things come in threes. Try this fun game of threes with your child!

Materials:
- Magazines with lots of pictures
- Scissors
- Small envelopes
- Sheet of paper and felt-tip pens (optional)

Learning Skills:	• Classification skills • Cognitive/thinking skills • Language and vocabulary development • Math/counting skills • Social interaction

What to Do:
1. Find magazine pictures of items that go together in threes such as three toppings on a pizza, three clothing items in an outfit, three features on a face, three people in a family, and so on.

2. Cut out the items and organize them into groups of threes.

3. Place the groups in envelopes and stack them on a table.

4. Have your child select an envelope, remove one picture, and tell you what it is.

5. Ask her what the other two pictures inside the envelope might be.

6. Have her remove another picture.

7. Discuss how the two pictures are alike.

8. Ask her what she thinks the next picture will be.

9. Have her remove the last picture.

10. Ask her how the three items go together.

11. Repeat with the remaining envelopes.

Variation: Give your child a turn to collect three items and have you guess how they go together!

Caution: Make sure she's careful around the scissors.

TOOTHPICK-TURES

Your child can make pictures out of many different materials. See what he comes up with using only toothpicks!

Materials:
- Plain and colored toothpicks
- Construction paper (optional)
- Table
- Glue

Learning Skills:	• Cognitive/thinking skills • Creativity and imagination • Emotional expression • Fine motor development

What to Do:

1. Pour some toothpicks on a table.

2. Seat your child at the table and ask him to design a picture using the toothpicks.

3. If he needs help getting started, show him how to move the toothpicks around to make shapes, designs, people, animals, and so on.

4. Admire his picture after he finishes.

5. Have him glue his toothpick-ture to a sheet of construction paper if he likes.

Variation: Add play dough to the mix and let him connect the toothpicks with the dough.

Caution: Tell him to be careful handling the toothpicks since they have sharp ends.

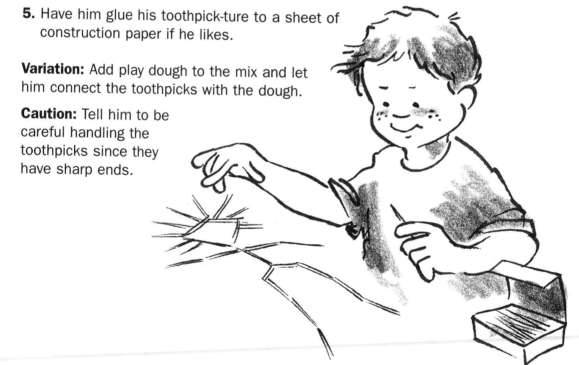

128

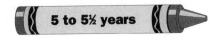
WALK ON THE WILD SIDE

Here's a game that allows your child's mind and body to make-believe together!

Materials:
- Large area
- 5-foot length of rope

<table>
<tr><td rowspan="7">**Learning Skills:**</td><td>• Cause and effect</td></tr>
<tr><td>• Cognitive/thinking skills</td></tr>
<tr><td>• Creativity and imagination</td></tr>
<tr><td>• Gross motor development</td></tr>
<tr><td>• Language and vocabulary development</td></tr>
<tr><td>• Problem solving</td></tr>
<tr><td>• Social interaction</td></tr>
</table>

What to Do:

1. Find a large area where your child can walk around freely.

2. Lay the rope down in a straight line with plenty of room all around it.

3. Have your child stand at one end of the rope path.

4. Tell her she has to walk across the path imagining that it's made out of ice. Have her walk in a way that's appropriate for ice.

5. When she reaches the other side, have her return along the path imagining it's made out of hot coals.

6. Continue imagining surfaces for her to walk on, and have her create a walk that's appropriate for each surface. You might consider soft grass, deep sand, slimy mud, prickly pine needles, deep snow, sticky glue, and so on.

Variation: Have your child take off her shoes and close her eyes as she walks, so she has to keep on the path by feel alone.

Caution: Make sure the area is clear so your child doesn't bump into anything.

129

WHAT HAPPENS NEXT?

Help your child learn how to anticipate things and predict consequences with a game of What Happens Next?

Materials:
- Magazine with lots of pictures or an inexpensive picture book
- Cozy chair

Learning Skills:	• Cognitive/thinking skills • Emotional expression • Language and vocabulary development • Self-awareness • Social interaction

What to Do:

1. Sit in a cozy chair with your child so that both of you can see the magazine.

2. Open to the first interesting picture.

3. Discuss with him what's happening in the picture.

4. Ask him to imagine what might happen next.

5. When you finish, turn the page to find other interesting pictures to talk about.

Variation: Read a picture book and ask your child, "What's going to happen next?" before you turn each page.

Caution: Make sure the magazine doesn't contain any disturbing images.

5½ TO 6 YEARS

As your child reaches school age, there will be an explosion of physical, cognitive, and social abilities. All the skills she's learned so far will be building blocks for future learning. Continue to provide experiences that will enrich her language skills, cognitive abilities, and social awareness. Here are ways to further enhance her overall development:

- Read to your child often, act out the stories you've read, guess the endings to stories, and draw pictures to go along with the tales. These activities help prepare your child for those first reading and writing experiences by further expanding her vocabulary and language skills.

- Give your child every opportunity to gain confidence in her cognitive skills—the key to success in school. And offer lots of ways to enhance your child's social skills—the key to success in life.

- Let your child have lots of free time, space, and materials to practice her exploding physical skills. Teach her new skills when she's ready.

- Encourage creative thinking and let your child try to solve her own problems. Give her assistance as needed without fixing problems for her. Ask your child questions to get her started.

- Provide your child with numerous opportunities for social interaction, so she'll continue to learn to get along with others. Encourage cooperation, sharing, and enjoying the company of friends.

- Round out your child's overall growth and development the same way you started it: by simply playing together!

ACT iT OUT

Your child can talk, but can she express herself in other ways? Try a game of Act It Out!

Materials:
- Picture books

What to Do:

1. Let your child select a picture book she'd like to act out. Tell her to keep her selection a secret.

Learning Skills:	• Cognitive/thinking skills
	• Dramatic play
	• Emotional expression
	• Problem solving
	• Self-awareness
	• Social interaction

2. When she's ready, ask her to tell you what the story was about—without talking! She must act out the story without words, and you must try to understand what she's trying to express.

3. As your child acts out the story, say the words that explain what she's doing.

4. When you finish, read the book together and see how much you got right.

Variation: Ask your child to act out other things such as her day at preschool, a movie she has seen, a story about a family member, and so on.

Caution: Have your child pick a story very familiar to her, so she doesn't have trouble understanding what to act out.

DIGGING!

ALL MiXED UP

Your child is becoming more logical, so play a game of All Mixed Up to see if he can figure out what's wrong.

Materials:
- Several items that go together such as the ingredients of a sandwich, articles of an outfit, pieces of a puzzle, and so on

Learning Skills:
- Cause and effect
- Cognitive/thinking skills
- Language and vocabulary development
- Problem solving
- Social interaction

What to Do:

1. Gather the necessary items for an activity.

2. Begin the activity—but do something that isn't right and see if your child notices. For example, if you make a sandwich, say, "First spread the bread on the peanut butter."

3. He should say, "That's all mixed up!"

4. Continue working on the task, doing some things right and some things wrong. Encourage him to catch you when you make mistakes.

5. Let your child take a turn mixing things up and see if you can catch him!

Variation: Tell a story and get it all mixed up. Have your child tell you what's wrong and see if he can remember how the story goes.

Caution: If your child is confused or frustrated, provide lots of clues and encouragement.

THAT'S NOT RIGHT!

BLiND WALK

Take your child on a Blind Walk so she can gain a new perspective on her world!

Materials:
- Nature area
- Blindfold (optional)

Learning Skills:
- Cognitive/thinking skills
- Mental imagery
- Problem solving
- Sensory awareness
- Social interaction
- Spatial awareness

What to Do:
1. Find a nature area to explore together.

2. Tell your child to keep her eyes closed and trust you. A blindfold would work best, if she's willing.

3. Have her hold your hand as you walk.

4. Encourage her to talk about what she hears, smells, and feels.

5. Stop along the path occasionally and have her touch a tree, rock, flower, and so on.

6. Have her describe what she feels and guess what it might be. Tell her if she's right!

7. Keep walking, making sure your child is comfortable, and have her perceive all the things around her without using her sense of sight.

Variation: Let your child lead you on a Blind Walk, but remind her to avoid dangerous objects.

Caution: Watch out for anything that might hurt or startle her such as overhanging branches, narrow paths, rocks, critters, and so on.

CLOCKWORKS

Look for an old clock or other mechanical device tucked away in the garage or attic. Your child will have fun finding out what makes it tick!

Materials:
- Old clock or other mechanical device that can be taken apart safely
- Table or floor
- Screwdriver and other simple tools

Learning Skills:
- Cause and effect
- Cognitive/thinking skills
- Fine motor development
- Language and vocabulary development
- Problem solving
- Social interaction

What to Do:
1. Find an old clock or buy one at a local thrift shop.
2. Place it on a table or floor.
3. Give your child a screwdriver and a few other simple tools.
4. Ask him to take apart the clock.
5. Have him try to figure out how to do it. Provide clues if necessary.
6. When the parts are removed, discuss what they do and how the clock works.

Variation: Have your child try to put the clock together again, or select another simple device for him to take apart.

Caution: Make sure he's careful with the tools and sharp edges.

COLOR CALLS

Your child is learning how symbols express meaning with gestures, language, and prewriting skills. She'll have fun expressing meaning with colors!

Materials:
- 1 sheet each of red, blue, yellow, and green construction paper
- Felt-tip pens or crayons (optional)
- Large play area

Learning Skills:	• Cognitive/thinking skills
	• Gross motor development
	• Mental imagery
	• Social interaction

What to Do:

1. Find four sheets of colored construction paper—red, blue, yellow, and green— or have your child make them using white paper and felt-tip pens or crayons.

2. Find a large area where your child can run around.

3. Explain to her that each time you hold up a color, she must perform a task associated with that color. For example, if you hold up the red paper, she must jump; if you hold up blue, she must run; and so on.

4. Have your child stand in the middle of the play area.

5. Hold up one of the colored papers and have her perform the appropriate action.

6. Hold up another color. She must switch immediately to that action.

7. Continue holding up the colors, changing the action, until she's tired!

Variation: Add more colors and more tasks to make the game more challenging.

Caution: Go slowly at first so your child doesn't get tired too quickly.

DRAW TO MUSIC

It's relaxing to draw to music. It's also educational and gives your child the opportunity to express himself in different ways.

Materials:
- Cassette player with several varieties of prerecorded music
- Drawing pad
- Felt-tip pens or crayons

Learning Skills:	• Cognitive/thinking skills • Creativity and imagination • Emotional expression • Self-awareness/self-esteem • Social interaction

What to Do:
1. Tape-record several varieties of music such as classical, country and western, pop, rock, hip-hop, children's tunes, and so on. Record one to three minutes of each variety.

2. Provide your child with a pad of drawing paper and felt-tip pens or crayons.

3. Turn on the music and tell him to draw whatever comes to mind!

4. When the music changes, have your child turn the page and begin a new drawing inspired by the different music.

5. Repeat until the tape is finished.

6. Mix up his pictures and rewind the tape. Play it back and see if he can remember which picture goes with which type of music.

7. Have your child talk about how each type of music made him feel.

Variation: Make a tape with other sounds that are not necessarily musical such as engines running, water flowing, birds chirping, and so on. Repeat the steps above to see what your child will create.

Caution: Don't play anything too depressing or difficult to follow.

FACE iT

Have fun mixing up facial parts to create funny-looking people, then have your child try to restore the faces to their original appearance.

Materials:
- Magazines with large pictures of faces
- Scissors
- Glue or tape
- Construction paper

Learning Skills:
- Classification skills
- Cognitive/thinking skills
- Fine motor development
- Mental imagery
- Problem solving
- Self-awareness/self-image

What to Do:

1. Cut out large faces from magazines.

2. Cut out the eyes, noses, and mouths, and separate these into piles.

3. Glue or tape the remaining facial parts to pieces of construction paper.

4. Next, place the wrong eyes, noses, and mouths on the various faces.

5. Have your child look at the funny faces you made!

6. Ask her if she can figure out what parts belong to what face.

7. Have her rearrange the facial features until they're restored to their original appearances.

8. Glue on the parts to make the faces complete again.

Variation: Let your child take a turn selecting and mixing up the face parts for you.

Caution: Handle scissors carefully.

FEELY BAGS

Preschool-age children learn a great deal with their senses. Help develop your child's sense of touch with a game of Feely Bags.

Materials:
- 6 to 8 paper bags
- 6 to 8 items to feel such as a sponge, ball of clay, handful of rubber bands, sheet of sandpaper, sticky candy, glob of Slime, package bow, flower, and so on
- Floor or table

Learning Skills:
- Classification skills
- Cognitive/thinking skills
- Language and vocabulary development
- Mental imagery
- Sensory awareness
- Social interaction

What to Do:
1. Place each item in a paper bag and fold the top.
2. Place the bags on the floor or table between you and your child.
3. Have him choose a bag, open the top, and stick his hand inside without looking.
4. Instead of asking him to name the item, ask him to describe how the item feels in as much detail as possible.
5. When he finishes his description, you should try to guess the item.
6. Have your child remove the item from the bag to see if you were right!
7. Continue playing with the other bags.

Variation: Have your child collect things for you to feel and describe, so he can guess!

Caution: Choose items that can be handled safely.

FINGER GOLF

Your child's fingers are getting better and better at following her commands. She'll enjoy her manual dexterity with a fun game of Finger Golf!

Materials:
- Large play area
- Ping-Pong balls or golf balls
- 6 sheets of green construction paper
- Scissors
- Black felt-tip pen
- Double-stick tape

Learning Skills:	• Cause and effect • Cognitive/thinking skills • Eye-hand coordination • Fine motor development • Math/counting skills • Problem solving • Social interaction

What to Do:

1. Find a large area for playing.

2. Make golf course greens by rounding pieces of green construction paper with scissors.

3. Number each green and draw a hole in the middle of each one about three inches in diameter.

4. Position the greens around the room in consecutive order a few feet apart.

5. Secure the greens to the floor with double-stick tape.

6. Place double-stick tape on each hole to catch the ball.

7. Place your golf or Ping-Pong balls a few feet from the first hole.

8. Take turns using your fingers to swing at the balls and move them toward the first hole.

9. Take turns pushing the ball toward the hole until you both reach it.

10. Repeat with the other holes.

Variation: Set up a peewee golf course in the back yard for fun gross motor development. Use plastic clubs and balls and be creative designing holes!

Caution: Be careful not to flick your finger too hard—it can hurt!

FLEA CIRCUS

...e game that enhances your child's imag-...

Learning Skills:	• Cognitive/thinking skills
	• Creativity and imagination
	• Fine motor development
	• Social interaction

...truction paper to form your three-ring circus.

...near each other.

...rings.

...nd the performers are so tiny you can hardly see them.

...on, use your finger to point out the different flea acts. For example, you might say, "Here comes the flea lion and over there is the flea tamer. Now watch the flea lion jump through the hoop! Wow, he made it! The flea tamer is giving the lion a snack for doing such a good job! Look! Here come the flea clowns! Look at that silly one doing somersaults!" Keep moving your finger as you describe the performances so your child can follow along in his imagination.

...pening at the flea circus, using his finger to point out the different acts.

Variation: Create other miniature events and have your child imagine what's happening.

Caution: If your child becomes confused or frustrated, re-mind him it's only make-believe.

141

HANDS AND FEET

Your child can tell her hands from her feet, but can she tell her handprints from her footprints? She'll have fun following the Hands and Feet path!

Materials:
- Construction paper
- Felt-tip pen
- Scissors
- Double-stick tape

Learning Skills:	• Cognitive/thinking skills • Fine and gross motor development • Problem solving • Self-awareness • Spatial relationships

What to Do:

1. Using a felt-tip pen, draw outlines of your child's hands and bare feet on construction paper. Cut out the outlines to make handprints and footprints.

2. Make several duplicates of the prints.

3. Place double-stick tape on the backs of the prints.

4. Stick them to the floor, forming a path from one end of the room to the other.

5. Have your child place her foot on the first footprint or her hand on the first handprint. Make sure she selects the appropriate side—left or right—as required.

6. Have her continue along the path, placing her hands and feet on the appropriate prints, until she reaches the end!

Variation: To make the game more challenging, place the prints farther apart.

Caution: In the first game, make sure the prints are close enough for your child to reach easily.

142

"i CAN!" CHART

Help your child appreciate how many things he can do by making an "I CAN!" chart that highlights his accomplishments each week.

Materials:
- Poster board
- Ruler
- Felt-tip pens
- Stickers or stars

Learning Skills:	• Cognitive/thinking skills • Fine and gross motor development • Problem solving • Self-awareness/self-esteem

What to Do:

1. Make the chart by drawing grid lines on a piece of poster board.

2. Write "I CAN!" at the top.

3. Down the left side, list several tasks your child can already do such as "Brush my teeth," "Get myself dressed," "Feed the dog," and so on.

4. Each week, add a new task that your child has accomplished. Review all the items occasionally so your child can appreciate his achievements!

Variation: List the new tasks you want your child to accomplish in the future, and help him work toward those goals. Each time he succeeds, add the item to his "I CAN!" chart.

Caution: Try to find at least one task per week that your child has accomplished, even if it's something small. Every major achievement begins with a small step!

MAGIC LETTERS

With a little imagination, your child will enjoy turning ordinary alphabet letters into magical pictures.

Materials:
- Table
- Pad of drawing paper
- Felt-tip pens or crayons

What to Do:

1. Sit at a table with your child.

2. Ask her to name a letter of the alphabet.

Learning Skills:	• Cognitive/thinking skills • Creativity and imagination • Eye-hand coordination • Fine motor development • Language and vocabulary development • Prereading skills • Prewriting skills • Social interaction

3. Write the letter in large print in the middle of the paper.

4. Slide the paper over to her and have her transform the letter into a funny picture of an animal, design, or other object.

5. Select another letter and repeat.

Variation: Select a number or other symbol and have your child turn it into a funny picture!

Caution: Make the letter big enough to allow plenty of room for your child's creativity.

MAKE A CHAIN

Have your child make a colorful paper chain to count off the days before a special event!

Materials:
- Colored construction paper cut into 1-by-4-inch strips
- Scissors
- Felt-tip pens or stickers
- Calendar
- Tape or glue

Learning Skills:	• Cognitive/thinking skills • Fine motor development • Math/counting skills • Mental imagery

What to Do:

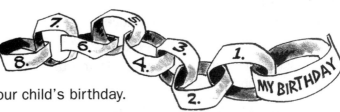

1. Choose a special calendar date such as a holiday or your child's birthday.

2. Help your child count the number of days until the special event.

3. Cut out this number of paper strips. Make sure to add one for the special day.

4. Label the special-day strip and number the rest in ascending order beginning with 1.

5. Show your child how to make chain links by looping the special-day strip to form a ring, then gluing or taping the ends together.

6. Select the strip labeled 1 and run it through the special-day link before taping the ends together.

7. Continue connecting the numbered strips in ascending order.

8. Have your child remove the highest-numbered link each day by tearing the strip in half. He will always know how many days remain until the special event!

Variation: Make a candy or cereal necklace and let your child eat one item each day.

Caution: Tape is easier than glue for this project. Always be careful with scissors around your child.

145

NO HANDS!

Your child is becoming quite skilled at using her hands, so give her a task where she can't use them and see how she solves the problem!

Materials:
- Supplies for a task such as a wash-cloth to wash her face, sock to put on her foot, sandwich to eat, and so on

Learning Skills:
- Cause and effect
- Cognitive/thinking skills
- Creativity and imagination
- Gross motor development
- Problem solving
- Self-awareness/body image

What to Do:

1. Choose a challenging yet manage-able task that your child can perform without her hands.

2. Let her figure out how to complete the task. She might use her teeth, her feet, her head, and so on.

3. Watch her carefully as she figures out the various problems, praising her as she solves each part of the challenge!

4. When she finishes, have her clap and yell, "Look, Mom, no hands!"

Variation: Have your child put her arms behind her back. Sit behind her and slip your arms into her arm spaces. Have her perform a task using your hands instead of hers by explaining what needs to be done!

Caution: Make sure the task isn't too diffi-cult, and watch that she doesn't do any-thing dangerous to solve her problem.

NOISEMAKER

Children love to make noises, and your child will have fun guessing what noise you make!

Materials:
- Noise-making objects such as a door-bell, cat, water faucet, vacuum cleaner, telephone, typewriter, train, car engine, flushing toilet, and so on
- Table or floor
- Blindfold (optional)
- Tape recorder and tape (optional)
- Quiet room

Learning Skills:	• Cognitive/thinking skills • Listening/sound discrimination • Mental imagery • Social interaction

DING·DONG!

What to Do:

1. Make a list of several noise-making items familiar to your child. You might also want to record various sounds on tape before starting the game.

2. Sit with your child at a table or on the floor in a quiet room and ask him to listen carefully. Blindfold him or have him close his eyes so he cannot see what you do.

3. Make the sound of one of the items on your list.

4. Ask your child to guess the item. Give him hints if necessary.

5. Repeat with the rest of the sounds.

Variation: Cut out pictures to match the sounds, spread them on the floor or table, and let your child match the sound to the picture. Or, have him take a turn making sounds for you to guess.

Caution: Avoid loud sounds that might startle your child or hurt his ears.

OBJECT OUTLINE

Can your child tell what an object is by looking at its outline? Find out with this fun game!

Materials:
- Several objects with well-defined outlines such as a cookie cutter, fork, ball, action figure, shoe, toy car, pencil, toothbrush, and so on
- Construction or drawing paper
- Fine felt-tip pen
- Paper bag

Learning Skills:	• Cognitive/thinking skills • Language and vocabulary development • Mental imagery • Problem solving/deductive reasoning • Social interaction

What to Do:
1. Select several items that have well-defined outlines.

2. Place each item on a separate sheet of paper and draw its outline with a fine felt-tip pen.

3. Gather the outlines in a pile and place the items in a paper bag.

4. Call your child into the room.

5. Show her the first outline and have her guess the item. Give her hints if necessary.

6. After she guesses correctly, pull the item out of the bag and place it on the outline!

7. Repeat for the remaining items.

Variation: After your child guesses the item, have her draw the details into the outline. Or, have your child draw outlines for you to guess.

Caution: Make sure to use items that are safe to handle.

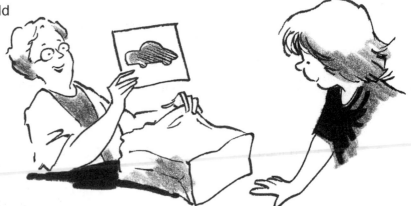

PAPER-BAG HEAD

Your child will have fun seeing the world in a whole new way—with a paper bag over his head!

Materials:
- Large paper bag
- Table
- Felt-tip pens, crayons, stickers, and other items to decorate the bag
- Scissors

Learning Skills:	• Cognitive/thinking skills • Problem solving • Self-awareness • Sensory awareness • Spatial relationships

What to Do:

1. Lay a paper bag flat on a table with the flap facing down.

2. Have your child color and decorate the bag to make a human head, monster head, robot head, and so on.

3. Cut eyeholes in the bag.

4. Let your child walk around the house or yard with the bag over his head, looking out through the eyeholes.

5. Ask him what it's like to walk around with a paper-bag head!

Variation: To make the game more challenging, place the bag over your child's head without cutting eyeholes. Watch him carefully as he walks around, since he can only see down.

Caution: Make sure the area is clear of dangerous items, and watch your child closely as he moves through the house or yard.

PiCK 'EM UP

Offer your child an opportunity to sharpen her fine motor skills with this fun game!

Materials:
- Uncarpeted floor or table
- Plastic drinking straws

Learning Skills:	• Cause and effect • Cognitive/thinking skills • Fine motor development • Problem solving • Social interaction

What to Do:
1. Sit on an uncarpeted floor or at a table.

2. Gather several drinking straws and have your child hold them straight up in the middle of the floor or table.

3. Let her release the straws and watch them tumble all around.

4. Take turns removing straws from the jumbled pile, one at a time, without moving any of the other straws.

5. A player gets to keep a straw if she removes it without moving any of the other straws.

6. If you disturb another straw, your turn is over and you leave the straw on the pile.

7. Continue playing until all the straws are picked up.

Variation: To make the game more challenging, play with toothpicks.

Caution: Be careful with toothpicks so you don't get pricked!

SIMPLE SIMON SAYS

Play this popular game with your preschooler—on a simpler level, of course!

Materials:
• Large area for playing

Learning Skills:	• Cognitive/thinking skills • Fine and gross motor development • Language and vocabulary development • Listening skills • Self-awareness • Social interaction

What to Do:

1. Stand facing your child.

2. Say the words "Simon says," then instruct your child to perform some type of body movement. Demonstrate the movement while giving the command.

3. Explain to your child that he's only supposed to follow your instruction if you say the words "Simon says" first.

4. After three or four commands, try to trick him by not saying "Simon says" before giving a command. He should refuse to do the movement because you didn't say "Simon says."

5. If he follows correctly, continue playing.

6. If he gets it wrong, let him take a turn being Simon.

Variation: Instead of saying "Simon Says," simply give and perform commands. Try to trick your child by giving a command but doing something different, and see if he catches you.

Caution: Maintain a slow pace at first so your child can process the instructions without getting frustrated.

SUPERHERO COSTUME

You can turn any ordinary kid into a superhero with a towel and safety pins!

Materials:
- Colorful towel or piece of fabric to form a cape
- 2 safety pins
- Colorful socks, tights, paper crown, mask, gloves, and T-shirt with emblem (optional)

Learning Skills:
- Cognitive/thinking skills
- Creativity and imagination
- Dramatic play
- Emotional expression
- Language and vocabulary development
- Self-awareness/self-esteem

What to Do:

1. Gather the materials you want to use for your child's superhero costume.

2. Attach a cape or towel to the back of her shirt with safety pins.

3. Let her add other accessories if she likes.

4. Tell her to think of a name for her new superhero character.

5. Ask her what super powers she has and what she can do that others can't!

6. Turn her loose to save the day!

Variation: Set up a cardboard playhouse for your superhero's fort.

Caution: Tell your child it's only make-believe and not to try anything dangerous!

TALKiNG TiME

When two people take turns talking, it's called conversation. When two people talk at the same time, it's called Talking Time!

Materials:
- 2 magazines with lots of pictures
- Floor or table

Learning Skills:	• Cognitive/thinking skills • Language and vocabulary development • Listening skills • Memory enhancement • Social interaction

What to Do:
1. Give one magazine to your child and keep the other for yourself.

2. Sit on the floor or at a table and open the magazines, keeping the pages hidden from one another.

3. Have your child choose a picture to talk about, and choose one yourself.

4. Set a timer for thirty seconds.

5. At the word "Go," begin talking about your pictures at the same time!

6. Try to listen to what the other person is saying while you talk.

7. When time is up, describe what you heard the other person say.

8. Show your picture to the other person to find out if he heard correctly.

Variation: Tell stories based on a specific topic. Follow steps 4 through 8.

Caution: Shorten the time if your child gets frustrated.

" AND THE WATERFALL POURED OVER..." "...THE PUPPY WITH BROWN EYES."

TREASURE MAP

Can your child find a treasure hidden in her own house? A treasure map will help!

Materials:
- Sheet of construction paper
- Felt-tip pens
- Prize or treat

Learning Skills:
- Cognitive/thinking skills
- Following directions
- Mental imagery
- Problem solving
- Spatial relationships

What to Do:

1. Draw a map of the inside of your house.

2. Show it to your child and have her walk through the house using the map to see how the rooms are represented on the paper.

3. Hide a snack or treat in one of the rooms and mark the treasure on the map.

4. Give your child the map again and see if she can find the treasure!

Variation: Let your child hide something for you to find.

Caution: Be sure to hide the treat in a safe place.

VOLLEY BALLOON

Have your child work off some energy by batting around a balloon that keeps falling to the ground!

Materials:
- Large play area
- Blown-up balloons

Learning Skills:	• Body awareness
	• Cause and effect
	• Cognitive/thinking skills
	• Gross motor development
	• Spatial relationships

What to Do:

1. Find a wide-open space where you can bat a balloon without worrying about crashing into anything.

2. Hit the balloon up in the air toward your child.

3. As the balloon falls to the ground, have your child hit it up in the air back toward you.

4. Try to keep the balloon up in the air as long as you can, batting it back and forth.

Variation: Give each player a balloon and have him try to keep his balloon up in the air as long as possible.

Caution: Be sure the area is clear so you don't bump into anything.

YARN WEB

Have your child follow the yarn web that takes her body up and down and all around!

Materials:
- Colorful yarn

What to Do:

1. Buy a skein of colorful yarn.

2. Begin unraveling the yarn at one end of a room, securing it around a doorknob.

Learning Skills:	• Body awareness • Cause and effect • Cognitive/thinking skills • Gross motor development • Problem solving • Spatial relationships

3. Continue unraveling the yarn as you walk around the room, winding it around various pieces of furniture.

4. Find a spot to end the trail.

5. Bring your child to the door and show her the web of yarn.

6. Show her where it begins and tell her to follow the yarn all the way to the end. Have her gather it as she goes!

Variation: Have a small treat or prize waiting for her when she gets to the end.

Caution: Avoid winding the yarn around lamps or other loose, breakable items.

INDEX

T

V

W

Y

Baby Play & Learn

by Penny Warner

Child development expert Penny Warner offers 160 ideas for games and activities that will provide hours of developmental learning opportunities, including bulleted lists of skills that your baby learns through play, step-by-step instructions for each game and activity, and illustrations demonstrating how to play many of the games.

Order #1275

Parent-Tested Ways to Grow Your Child's Confidence

by Silvana Clark

In this book you'll find 150 tested ideas designed to enhance your child's self-confidence. Discover great ways to share enjoyable moments together, teach important skills, celebrate special occasions, encourage creativity, and recognize achievements.

Order #1212

The Toddler's Busy Book

by Trish Kuffner

This book contains 365 activities (one for each day of the year) for toddlers using things found around the home. It shows parents and day-care providers how to prevent boredom, stimulate a child's natural curiosity, and keep toddlers occupied.

Order #1250

The Preschooler's Busy Book

by Trish Kuffner

This book contains 365 activities (one for each day of the year) for three- to six-year-olds using things found around the home. It shows parents and day-care providers how to prevent boredom, stimulate a child's natural curiosity, and keep toddlers occupied.

Order #6055

Fun Family Traditions

by Cynthia MacGregor

This book is packed with complete directions for fun and meaningful family activities—all designed to strengthen families and help instill feelings of love, belonging, and family pride.

Order #2446

Practical Parenting Tips

by Vicki Lansky

Here's the #1-selling tricks-of-the-trade book for new parents. Includes tips on toilet training, discipline, travel, temper tantrums, childproofing, and more.

Order # 1180

Discipline without Shouting or Spanking

by Jerry Wyckoff, Ph.D., and Barbara C. Unell

The most practical guide to discipline available, this book provides proven methods for handling the 30 most common forms of childhood misbehavior, from whining and temper tantrums to sibling rivalry.

Order #1079

What Do You Know about Manners?

by Cynthia MacGregor

Here is a book about manners that kids will actually enjoy reading! And their parents will love it, too. It's filled with fun, imaginative ways to fine-tune a child's manners and contains over 100 quiz items and hilarious illustrations.

Order #3201

Feed Me I'm Yours

by Vicki Lansky

Parents love this easy-to-use, economical guide to making baby food at home. More than 200 recipes cover everything a parent needs to know about teething foods, nutritious snacks, and quick, pleasing lunches. Comb-bound for easy use.

Order #1109

Healthy Food for Healthy Kids

by Bridget Swinney, M.S., R.D.

Here is *the* parents' practical guide to selecting and cooking healthy meals for kids and to creating healthy attitudes toward food. More than just a cookbook, this is a user-friendly book with real-world advice for parents who want their children to eat better.

Order #1129

Look for Meadowbrook Press books where you buy books. You may also order books by using the form printed below.

Qty.	Title	Author	Order No.	Unit Cost (U.S. $)	Total
	Order Form				
	Baby/Child Emergency First Aid	Einzig, M.	1381	$8.00	
	Baby & Child Medical Care	Einzig/Hart	1159	$9.00	
	Baby Play & Learn	Warner, P.	1275	$9.00	
	Child Care A to Z	Woolfson, R.	1010	$11.00	
	Childhood Medical Record Book	Fix, S.	1130	$10.00	
	Dads Say the Dumbest Things!	Lansky/Jones	4220	$7.00	
	Discipline w/o Shouting/Spanking	Wyckoff/Unell	1079	$6.00	
	Feed Me! I'm Yours	Lansky, V.	1109	$9.00	
	First-Year Baby Care	Kelly, P.	1119	$10.00	
	Fun Family Traditions	MacGregor, C.	2446	$9.00	
	Gentle Discipline	Lighter, D.	1085	$6.00	
	Grandma Knows Best	McBride, M.	4009	$7.00	
	Healthy Food for Healthy Kids	Swinney, B.	1129	$12.00	
	How to Read Child Like a Book	Weiss, L.	1145	$8.00	
	Joy of Parenthood	Blaustone, J.	3500	$7.00	
	Kids' Party Games and Activites	Warner, P.	6095	$12.00	
	Kids' Pick-a-Party Book	Waner, P.	6090	$9.00	
	Moms Say the Funniest Things!	Lansky, B.	4280	$7.00	
	Parent-Tested/Child's Confidence	Clark, S.	1212	$8.00	
	Practical Parenting Tips	Lansky, V.	1180	$8.00	
	Preschooler Play & Learn	Warner, P.	1276	$9.00	
	Preschooler's Busy Book	Kuffner, T.	6055	$9.95	
	Toddler's Busy Book	Kuffner, T.	1250	$9.95	
	What Do You Know about Manners?	MacGregor, C.	3201	$6.99	
				Subtotal	
			Shipping and Handling (see below)		
			MN residents add 6.5% sales tax		
				Total	

YES! Please send me the books indicated above. Add $2.00 shipping and handling for the first book with a retail price up to $9.99 or $3.00 for the first book with a retail price over $9.99. Add $1.00 shipping and handling for each additional book. All orders must be prepaid. Most orders are shipped within 2 days by U.S. Mail (7–9 delivery days). Rush shipping is available for an extra charge. Overseas postage will be billed. **Quantity discounts available upon request.**

Send book(s) to:

Name _____ Address _____

City _____ State _____ Zip _____ Telephone (_____)_____

Payment via:

❏ Check or money order payable to Meadowbrook Press
❏ Visa (for orders over $10.00 only)   ❏ MasterCard (for orders over $10.00 only)

Account # _____ Signature _____ Exp. Date _____

A FREE Meadowbrook Press catalog is available upon request.
You can also phone us for orders of $10.00 or more at 800-338-2232.

Mail to: Meadowbrook Press, 5451 Smetana Drive, Minnetonka, MN 55343
Phone 952-930-1100   Toll-Free 800-338-2232   Fax 952-930-1940
For more information (and fun) visit our website: www.meadowbrookpress.com